REENGINEERING
MANAGEMENT

James Champy is the coauthor of
Reengineering the Corporation.

REENGINEERING MANAGEMENT

THE MANDATE FOR
NEW LEADERSHIP

JAMES CHAMPY

HarperBusiness
A Division of HarperCollinsPublishers

A hardcover edition of this book was published in 1995 by HarperBusiness, a division of HarperCollins Publishers.

HarperCollins books may be purchased for educational, business, or sales promotional use. For information please write: Special Markets Department, HarperCollins Publishers, Inc., 10 East 53rd Street, New York, NY 10022.

First paperback edition published 1996.

Designed by C. Linda Dingler

The Library of Congress has catalogued the hardcover edition as follows:

Champy, James, 1942–
    Reengineering management : the mandate for new leadership / James Champy. — 1st ed.
      p.   cm.
    Includes index.
    ISBN 0-88730-698-5
    1. Industrial management—United States. 2. Organizational change—United States. 3. Executives—United States. 4. Leadership. I. Title.
HD70.U5C49   1995
658.4'09—dc20   94-18739

ISBN 0-88730-796-5 (pbk.)
96 97 98 99 00 ❖/RRD 10 9 8 7 6 5 4 3 2 1

This book is dedicated
with love to my wife, Lois, and our
son, Adam.

"Things refuse to be mismanaged long."

—RALPH WALDO EMERSON

CONTENTS

ACKNOWLEDGMENTS

The revolution we started almost two years ago with the publication of *Reengineering the Corporation* continues only with the support of thousands of managers. My thanks to all of them for their contributions to the developing "science" of reengineering. My special thanks to the managers who participated in our research for this book. Their experiences and insights added much to the pages that follow. I can't thank them all individually, but I would like to single out a few: Dick Abdoo of Wisconsin Electric; Larry English of CIGNA HealthCare; Mark DeMichele of Arizona Public Service; Jim Olson of Hewlett-Packard; Mike Vinitsky of NutraSweet; and Rick Zaffarano of Hannaford Brothers.

I'm also grateful to the people with whom I have worked in developing the philosophy and practice of reengineering. They include: Tom Gerrity, now dean of the Wharton School of Business; Mike Hammer, coauthor of *Reengineering the Corporation*; and all of my associates at CSC, who continue to advance the practice of reengineering, including Gary Gulden, executive vice president of CSC Index, and Bob Morison, vice president of CSC's Research and Advisory Services.

For their role in the preparation of this book, my appreciation to Nelson W. Aldrich, Jr., Donna Sammons Carpenter, Sebastian Stuart, and the other talented writers, editors, and researchers at Wordworks, Inc.—Susan Buchsbaum, Maurice Coyle, Erik Hansen, Curtis Hartman, Martha Lawler, Mike Mattil, Cindy Sammons, and Charles Simmons. At Harper-

Collins, my thanks to: editor Adrian Zackheim, for his wisdom and help in focusing this book; to publisher Jack McKeown, for his continued support; and to publicist Lisa Berkowitz, for her enthusiasm in bringing this book to market.

I owe special thanks to Tom Waite, senior vice president of CSC Index, for his contribution to content and his critical role in bringing this book and the last from concept to reality. He has been the best of critics and the best of supporters. My thanks also to Sue Walseman of CSC Index and Bob Buday and Bob Gilbert of CSC for their efforts in the production and promotion of this work. Thanks, too, to Dee Dee Haggerty, for keeping my work organized. And for her continued guidance through the complexities of the publishing world (it must be reengineered!), I thank my agent, Helen Rees.

Finally, I must acknowledge my many "teachers" through the years, who both in the classroom and thereafter have stimulated my understanding and thinking on the work of managers. These include Tony Athos and Peter Drucker, who have inspired so many of us.

QUESTIONS THAT READERS ASK MOST

I have placed this chapter at the beginning of this paperback edition to give the reader a preview of what's to come. It contains some difficult questions asked by managers who are engaged in what often feels like a chaotic journey of change. My answers to these questions have evolved over time—and may continue to evolve as we reinvent our businesses and reengineer our processes. You may choose to answer these questions differently, and that's okay—because what's really important is the debate that we have. Our work should be affected by the Austrian philosopher Karl Popper's reminder of our managerial vulnerability: "I may be wrong, and you may be right. But by an effort, together, we may discover the truth."

The new edition of *Reengineering Management,* with this additional chapter, affords me the opportunity to incorporate a number of things I've learned since the book was first published. Most important, it allows me to address those questions most frequently raised in my discussions with managers and by readers of the first edition of *Reengineering Management* who have written letters and comments. Experience tells me that if a number of people have asked a question, many more will be interested in its answer. In addition, I hope to respond to some questions that were not asked but perhaps should have been. Like most authors, I have profited from the discussions that my work has inspired, and I welcome this opportunity to amplify and clarify some of my arguments. Even more, I hope that these questions will continue to promote a dialogue among managers about the nature of their own work. Since first writing *Reengineering Management*, I have become increasingly convinced that the real challenge to changing dramatically how companies operate is with managers, both in how they work and how they think.

In Reengineering Management you argue that, contrary to popular belief, a business is built not on numbers—bottom lines, market forces, production quotas—but on ideas and visions of what that business could be, what its managers want it to become. Yet managers at all levels often resist this process of constructing the future. What prevents managers from seeing into the future?

Two things chiefly. First, many managers, especially those in relatively successful businesses, naturally tend to keep tapping on the same old drum. After all, it's sounded the beat for lo these many generations, and the business keeps marching along in time. "Why argue with success?" they ask. In some ways these managers are what I'd call "too smart" for their own good; certainly too smart for the good of the business. They believe that they have had all the debates they need to have and that the industry will continue to exist as it has for many years. But what will they do, for instance, if they suddenly find the industry deregulated, and the business must be reconfigured in this deregulated environment? The questions they thought they had the answers to may no longer be the ones that people are asking. Perhaps these managers have been around the old industry simply too long to be able or willing to imagine that new configuration. They have failed to see that the debates really have to be about an entirely new industry context.

Some people in an industry have a sixth sense for industry change: They know that it's coming, and, what's more, they have an intuitive sense of how their business can reposition itself in order to take advantage of this industry change. This is where reengineering the business comes in, changing the fundamentals of the business by starting with the question, "*Why* are we doing what we are doing?" (I've called this the "purpose" question in this book.) Those managers who ask, "How can we do what we do better and faster?" are assuming that they can keep managing the business in pretty much the same old ways. When the business gets a little tough, they pull in their oars and float out the storm; when the sun comes out again, they go back to the same drumbeat. How many times have we seen this? When the business slumps, managers reduce costs in the belief that they will simply do less with less. A truly reengineered business, however, finds out how to do *more* with less.

Second, there is fear—fear of the unknown and its potential threats, its inevitable risks. Most of us, if we *really* face the future, are going to get a scare. A banker today ponders this thing called the "virtual bank"—no bricks, no mortar, just the network and the customers—and says, "That could happen this year in *my* market." It's in our human nature to want to deny inevitabilities and say, "that won't happen in *our* management lifetimes." But it could happen this year or next, and when it does, it will be a cataclysmic change for the industry and the way we do business.

In short, some managers are prevented from seeing the future because they are blinded by the sun of their current success and they cannot see the wall that they are driving right into. Also, I think many people suffer from a kind of subliminal denial of the future because to face it would be too traumatic.

If senior managers are entrenched, why don't boards of directors take action?

I think the way boards of directors operate today presents a crisis in management. That is, many directors fail to take action soon enough—or to inspire managers to take action soon enough—either when they anticipate business changes or when those changes suddenly appear before them like a brick wall as they are roaring down the highway. We have traditionally viewed boards as being relatively uninvolved in the day-to-day management of the business, and of course they *shouldn't* be involved.

The current crisis has complex causes. One problem we see so often is that board members don't understand the business well enough. Traditionally, we have gone outside the realm of the business to find board members—to academia, to the public sector, and to noncompeting industries. Furthermore, board members are subject to the approval of stockholders, who are, for the most part, loyal to the company but truly unaware of the big picture of what's happening in the industry. In a period of high industry change, businesses need board members who understand the quality and character of that change so that they can judge whether management is taking appropriate action, help and advise where appropriate, and take action if management is not.

Traditionally, boards of directors just haven't known enough about what's going on in the industry to accept the degree of accountability that managers and stockholders expect. Nor do they move fast enough when managers themselves fail to predict industry changes. Directors have a way out of this crisis if they are willing to "get smart" by asking questions about the business they direct and about the industry at large: How are they changing? What will customers need next year that they don't even know they will need? How is the business competitively distinctive, and is it maintaining that distinctiveness? A board can no longer be sure of a company's future success by the close review of quarterly financial reports. Its questions about where the industry is going must be far more probing.

Now, business and industry leadership usually originates at top management levels, i.e., with the company's chief executive officer or president. Boards must also increase their vigilance to be sure that they have a management leader in place.

Why are we seeing the elimination of so many middle-management positions? Isn't the corporation losing a lot of good people?

Many middle managers do their jobs very well, as we have defined them. So it's not really a question of performance. The real problem is not that the middle managers are disappearing, but that their jobs are: The work is simply evaporating. If you look carefully at this problem, you will discover at least three reasons for this change.

First, these middle-management positions give way in the general "flattening" of the corporation hierarchy that has been in vogue for the last few years.

Second, information technology has actually replaced or made obsolete the work traditionally done by some middle managers, a result that Peter Drucker predicted in his 1989 article "The Coming of a New Organization," in the *Harvard Business Review*. Drucker argued that middle-management positions would be replaced to a great degree by an information infrastructure, and we see that happening in all major industries today.

Third, *genuine* reengineering—not the superficial variety that many corporations present to their stockholders as evidence of greater austerity—has made much of the work of middle managers no longer relevant. In true reengineering, managerial accountability moves to the front line. Whatever supervisory capacity those middle managers might have had now passes to the people who work in teams or have become increasingly more *self-managed*.

Middle managers need to ask whether they can redefine their traditional role and the work they have done in order to add value to the business and its new definition of itself. If they take some stopgap alternative and simply join another company in the same middle-management capacity, they are merely postponing the inevitable. Sooner or later, the second corporation will undertake reengineering. Ultimately, middle-management work as we have traditionally known it will disappear altogether.

Many of the people who hold middle-management jobs are experienced and valuable to the business. When a business reengineers, it just may be the time for many of them to go back to doing real work—which companies should increasingly value and be willing to pay for.

If this part of the overall hierarchy collapses, it seems to follow that there will be no direct source within a company for developing managers. How do we train managers as the traditional structure falls?

The hierarchy did provide some structure for marking and noting levels of management skills as people moved into fixed positions and developed the skills they needed to function there. Today the development of managers, as it has been in some companies for some time, is more horizontal than vertical. We need to develop managers who are both broad in their experience and deep in their specialties. Breadth of experience comes when corporate executives encourage their managers to move into areas of the organization where they can gain experience and grow over time. Some people will resent this horizontal movement and interpret it as a mere transfer. If that's all it is, then the reengineering is already doomed. But if it's an opportunity for a manager to expand her knowledge of the corporation and develop skills that can increase the value-added contributions she makes to the organization, then the corporation will be doing itself and the manager a favor by enabling her to understand the different processes in how the company does business.

Also, we have already had enough experience to know that working in self-managed, process-oriented teams also increases managerial breadth and perspective. But there is no denying that the representation of the hierarchical structure of the organization, which oftentimes indicated the level of a person's skill, will have to be replaced by a much more accurately maintained description of an individual's real competencies.

What new job descriptions are being developed for these people?

In *Reengineering Management* I describe four managerial roles that a corporation needs to provide if it hopes to reengineer itself successfully. The *enterprise manager* is Argus-eyed: He or she sees with a hundred eyes what changes are coming and how they will wrench the corporation out of its rusty past. This person has traditionally been the CEO, but in tomorrow's successful organization he or she could rise from the ranks of management, having gained both breadth of experience and depth of specialty. The enterprise manager holds up both a mirror and a lamp to everyone connected with this company—directors, stockholders, employees, customers—both showing them what they are now and lighting the way to what they can become. In addition, we encourage enterprise managers to abandon the old management paradigm that they should be internally focused only. Managers need to look externally as well, particularly into the marketplace, where customers are real human beings rather than statistics on a shipping report.

The *expertise manager* takes responsibility for directing both the people and the technology that the corporation has gathered together to make its vision a reality. Every corporation has a number of people whose primary contributions reside in the expertise that they bring to their jobs: They know how to operate the billing processes or how information technology enables a new production line or how two new compounds produce a desired chemical reaction. But there needs to be someone, or a group of people, who can best coordinate these experts and the information that the technology allows them to produce. Moreover, the expertise manager has to be flexible and imaginative enough to allow people to experiment, innovate, and even to fail, for therein lies the future success of the corporation. In a world where, paradoxically, nothing is permanent except change itself, innovation is what keeps a business alive.

The *people* and *process managers* are those who are the best teachers, who recognize people's skills, and who enable them to contribute to the organization's processes rather than blocking their path to participation. Remember that reengineering the corporation most often means redefining our traditional notions of work and people: Rather than seeing them in terms of "tasks" quantitatively evaluated—How many buttons can they sew on in eight hours? How much money can be generated by shipping 1,000 cartons of computer software on Tuesday?— we need to see the corporation in terms of its *processes*, all the activities that the corporation undertakes to create value for its own people and its customers. The managers who take responsibility for these processes should be those who are the best enablers, the best coaches. Their highly developed networking skills allow them to bring people together in new and creative ways, people who used to work separately in walled-off departments but who now are free to move about and participate in making the decisions that affect their jobs and the future of the corporation.

Finally, everyone has to become a *self-manager,* accepting responsibility for performance and value-added contributions to the overall enterprise. This is where the idea of a corporate "culture" begins to come in. A culture is defined by its people, who establish and promote a set of collectively shared values. Self-management, taking responsibility for one's own performance and accepting the accountability that goes along with this freedom, is probably the single most important value that a corporation can promote during this period of change.

We've been talking about the company "culture" for a long time. Why are you emphasizing it so much now?

The truth is that it's been a lot of talk, but not much action, at least until recently. First, this word "culture" has to be clearly understood. I define it as a set of values shared broadly and deeply by people within the company, values that must be explicit and articulated repeatedly to ensure that people will do the right thing at the moment of truth. We can no longer assume that our culture will take care of itself, that it will be understood without reminding people in the organization why they are there doing what they do. Sometimes I hear that reengineering will make us all less dependent on others, but the opposite is true: As we reengineer the workplace, we in fact become increasingly *dependent* on people and on their capacity and willingness to do the right thing.

Reengineering gives people more control, more accountability, but without a rule book. No one can write a rule book to cover all the situations people will encounter; instead, we want to provide the operating principles that reflect the culture we want. In the end we must know—and this is largely a matter of faith—that people share these values deeply and that they will behave in the right way when put to the test.

How much articulation of the culture's value system do you need?

A corporation—indeed, an entire society—cannot afford to be ignorant of its culture. If the people who work and live in that culture cannot speak clearly and meaningfully about *why* they do what they do, then the culture is prone to corruption and disintegration. If a person knows that his organization values people who take chances in their innovations and that it does not punish an employee for a procedure that at first fails, he is going to come to value innovation and to recognize its rewards. If the organization has an appetite for change, a senior manager needs to understand what a difficult job she will have in uprooting the old processes, replacing them with more efficient configurations, and then maintaining and evaluating the changes as they progress. At every step she needs to remind herself and her teams that the organization supports this kind of activity.

If we give our people more freedom, how will we know that they will do the right thing?

As Socrates knew, there are many kinds or expressions of "right"—depending on what criteria one happens to be using. Sometimes there are conflicts: Doing the right thing that will increase profits may be the wrong thing to stimulate future growth or indeed may be entirely unethical or even illegal. This is why the *enterprise manager* is so important to successful reengineering, for this is the one person who has the vision and the hundred pairs of eyes to see that everyone is working in conjunction within the culture of the whole organization.

In our redefinition of managerial work, we need to develop new forms of *inspection,* a term I prefer instead of *control.* Old control systems no longer will work because we are not measuring the same things; for example, we are no longer solely evaluating performance quantitatively. To impose some form of hardline controls is completely contrary to enabling people to do the self-managed work we're asking them to perform. Managers need new ways of looking at the work their people are doing. I'm not talking about their acting like some hidden camera that swings 180° to record every movement, but suggesting that they hold daily or weekly conversations with their people and with their customers to determine that teams are working successfully together and that the organization is achieving its goals. In

Drucker's words, it's an extended version of managing by "walking around" though now, not just inside the company but outside the company, in its markets.

Ultimately, managers are accountable; thus, they have not only an obligation but also a responsibility to know. Walking the halls and walking in the marketplace will become increasingly important in this model of reengineered management. What better places are there to engage in conversation with employees and customers?

Shouldn't we try reengineering at a limited or protected area of the company to be sure that we don't risk the business?

I get that question all the time! People who ask it are probably those who touch the water with their toes to check its temperature. It's really a question about the scope of this thing we call the reengineered organization. If we're reengineering an order-fulfillment process, do we implement the changes only in one warehouse? Should we reengineer the photocopying department first so that if we fail, the entire business won't fall apart? That kind of questioning forces one to designate which parts of the body are "nonvital."

The analogy between the organization and the body is apt here. If you implant an organ, for example, the body can direct its antibodies on a search-and-destroy mission. Similarly, introduce a new process in one part of the business and more than likely it will be attacked as invasive and incompatible with the organization's image of itself. When this happens, you probably have not faced the larger group's cultural norms, the behavioral and style issues that underpin the organization's value system.

Contrary to what much experience and certainly much old wisdom tell us, the essence of reengineering lies in this principle: *The larger the scale of change, the greater the opportunity for success.* If you try to do this work incrementally, or if you try to shelter this work within a laboratory, particularly for too long a period of time, you will find that the organization as a whole will reject the new system.

When you face a large change—when you say you're going to make this change big time within the organization—you're forced to confront the larger issues of culture and management style that exist within the organization. The probability of success is higher if these larger issues are taken on directly than if you try to introduce change piecemeal. I know that this appears counterintuitive, but I'm increasingly convinced that this is correct.

How do we get senior managers to agree on a vision and to act?

One of the biggest challenges today occurs not in the middle of the organization, not deep in the organization, but at the level of the senior managers. I don't agree with the old song that people resist change. I think that people are fearful of change when they don't know where they're going, but they can get excited about these changes once they have a sense of where the whole operation is heading. We have to be realists and recognize that some people will leave the organization because of these changes. Some will move on because they disagree with the company's new direction; others, because the management structure has been rewritten. But those who remain with the company can and do become excited when they experience how their work takes on new meaning within the altered processes.

Although they appear entrenched, middle managers will ultimately have to follow the lead of the enterprise manager and accommodate themselves either within the new organizational structure or in another position outside the corporation. This change is inevitable and is guaranteed to be traumatic on a personal level, but there are ways of softening the blow if the organization helps the middle managers identify their real skills and make the appropriate transition to other work.

The biggest problem for reengineering, however, comes at the level of senior management. When genuine disagreement occurs at the top, senior managers often cannot agree on how to accomplish the goals or even what the goals are: Is it necessary to change the fundamental business model, to reinvent the business, or to reengineer the operating model? Having gained their positions because they knew how to operate within the old paradigm, these managers can have sharp disagreements with those who argue that radical change is imperative or that it must be accomplished quickly. Disagreements at this level and of this magnitude often result in utter silence, especially in organizations whose managers are "polite." Who would object to the proposition that Company X must be Number One in the industry or in the marketplace? Agreement is easy at this point because the proposition is still an abstraction; it can even be quite attractive. But when these senior managers start to deal with the reality of these broad statements, meetings often fracture along lines of deep disagreement. After the initial rumblings, there's an eerie silence. Then comes the panic when people think the entire organization is caving in around them.

If the organization needs reengineering, these big changes must be top-down and driven by those whose vision is the sharpest. If the senior managers do not agree, the change program will dwindle to nothing within a matter of months. If you are the company president or the CEO, you might have to realign some of the senior managers, especially those who are in deep denial and refuse to see the wall they are about to run into. At a minimum, you must have enough real debate with your managers to know where there is genuine disagreement.

What comes first, changing the way managers think or changing what managers do?

It's not a chicken-and-egg problem. Genuine reengineering occurs when these two processes are implemented at the same time. That said, however, I am convinced that managers do not respond well—none of us do—to a lot of conceptual managerial pronouncements. Starting the reengineering process by changing the *managerial work,* therefore, is going to have greater benefits for the organization. Once the managerial work is changed and a different managerial style is instituted—for example, replacing the watchdog model with the collaborative model—once people experience the differences in the decision processes associated with that work, then in time I believe we will get a change in managerial thought.

It's essential to distinguish between the process and the result: Changing worldviews—how we conceive of ourselves in relation to our work and to the larger group we work for or with—must take place over a long period of time. The end of this process will signal a truly new way of thinking about managing the organization. To make this distinction clearer, consider the process analogous to updating your software and reconfiguring your computer system. It takes a lot of time, and the process is rarely smooth and error-free, but in the end you have a new managerial system. Corporations, of course, are infinitely more complex, given that you are dealing with human feelings and seeking to establish collaborative relationships in this process. Managers are not plug-and-play devices to be reconfigured into the new system. Undertaking this process will not, in other words, be a quick fix: Count on the process taking five to twenty-five years, and build up a large supply of tolerance and patience.

Is this simply a generational issue? There are many people who say these old ways of thinking won't change until old managers die. I don't want to believe that. The push of technology itself—the way it has already affected the workplace, not to mention the wealth of changes in store for us—will force us to rethink our models for management. And the rate of industry change itself may not allow us the luxury of assuming that change in management work and thought will come on the next person's "watch."

What do you mean when you say that managers need to be "ambitious radicals?"

First, they are ambitious in setting radical *goals* for business change. They often throw shocking numbers onto the screen: Projected sales for new products, levels of customer service and satisfaction, costs, and the one that should appear on every quarterly report—revenue growth. When the organization sees these goals and the business case for change, it sees that it can no longer operate in the old way and that something big has to change if it is going to survive and prosper. The ambitious and radical goals actually help drive the change.

Second, managers need to be ambitious radicals about the *degree* of process change. The work models of the future will look nothing like the models we have now. And the success of these new models will be measured in both quantitative *and* qualitative terms. To prevent misunderstanding, let me say again that the reengineered organization must resist the temptation to identify output solely in quantitative terms.

How can we get people to participate in change programs if their jobs are at risk?

Everyone's job is at risk! It's important to keep saying this over and over: Reengineering is *not* a code word for laying off employees. There are a lot of people who want to interpret it that way. In order to get everyone involved in these change programs, we first have to persuade people that the company has *no choice* but to change. We have to put before them the "business case," as it has been called, along with its three components.

First, there is the picture of the industry as a whole. What are its projected movements? What are the inevitable changes? Where are the threats coming from? This big picture presents a tough sell, for people threatened with losing wages or jobs won't sit still for long while management talks in the abstract about industry trends and competition. Yet people must get some sense of these external forces if they are to understand the impetus for the internal changes.

Second, you have to locate the position of the organization in this industry-wide context. Establishing what's called the "case position" presents its own difficulties: You must first determine the important metrics by which to measure the business's performance; next, you must compare the business's performance record against those of its chief competitors and against the performance of companies outside your industry who may perform your core processes exceptionally well. And it's not enough to present this record in terms of last quarter's sales; rather, the organization's need for future growth may argue most effectively for deep changes, which, if they don't occur, may spell the end of the business. Furthermore, this projection capitalizes on the emotion of *fear*, in truth one of the key emotions that drives change.

Third, you must present a substantive operating vision.

Given current conditions and trends, how precise a picture of the future can you draw to describe the new operating model? Here the presence of the enterprise manager, the person who has the vision, becomes all-important. While we cannot displace fear, especially rational fears about job change or business "failure," no reengineering will get very far if that is the only emotion driving the change. An effective enterprise manager can inspire people with his vision and engage them in the change programs even though every job is on the line. If people suspect that in reality only *some* jobs are threatened, then the enterprise for change is at risk.

So we have to balance fear against hope?

Yes. In reality, the fear is there already. Now we have to counter that emotion with a vision that there's a powerful future for this business, and it will be a better place for people. In the end, some people will no longer be around. There is no way to engage the organization other than by persuading everyone that the company has no choice but to act.

How do you mobilize your organization and keep it mobilized for change?

Mobilization is a substantial part of management work now. I like to think in terms of three pieces of paper that I always have with me. On one piece, I describe the industry condition; the second provides a snapshot of the business within that industry; and the third piece of paper lays out a vision of the new operating model.

You keep an organization mobilized by constantly communicating and updating those three pieces of paper. And you try to live with one foot in the future and one in the present, consulting with the various constituencies to make sure they're doing what they need to do in order to bring about the change.

Think of those three pieces of paper together as a road map that keeps changing. Not only does it tell you where you have traveled in the past, but it keeps suggesting routes to follow and tries to show you, if you've got a traveler's eye, what roads are open down the way. Some may be interstate highways, fast and direct; others may offer a leisurely trip with scenic views. None will guarantee that you will not encounter roadblocks or wrecks along the way. Certainly, none will guarantee that you will arrive at the destination on time or even at all. The journey is everything—and your performance is being judged at all points along the journey.

This road map then is really a plan for instituting the changes?

Right. You start on this trip, and you discover things about your own condition and about the industry as you're making the changes. But no trip is entirely predictable; accordingly, the best traveler is the person or the organization that can revise its agenda as conditions warrant. You should not fool yourself by thinking that there is a single, fixed plan for change.

Nothing is permanent, and everyone must change, as you say in Reengineering Management. *You've talked about how long it will take an organization to institute a change in management thinking. How long do you think the change cycle itself will last?*

Anywhere from five to twenty-five years. Two main forces, among others, drive this change cycle: technology, particularly information technology, and the government's reassessing its role in business.

Advances in technology have allowed us to overproduce. Industries have achieved or are capable of achieving an overcapacity that will require from five to ten years to absorb. The technology keeps getting better and faster, and our operating procedures are always scrambling to keep up to date. Eventually they will settle down, although we shouldn't expect them ever to come to rest.

This change cycle is driven largely by the government as it reassesses its role in business. Recently we've seen legislation affecting deregulation, privatization, free trade, and a host of other issues. In addition, the government will demand that regulated industries, government companies, and privatized organizations compete and develop new ways of operating. Trade barriers will continue to fall, and the fundamental nature of competition will be redefined as new businesses enter our markets.

Make no mistake: Reengineering is not a fad. We may call it something else a few years from now, but we're going to keep making major operational changes and reinventing business for at least five, perhaps ten years. Some of my friends who are scientists make the generational argument that it will take at least twenty-five years for a new paradigm to be adopted and for the adherents to the old system to leave the scene. A conservative estimate, then, based on this premise, would place the change cycle at twenty-five years.

Given what appears to be an extended period of change, won't we burn out?

People burn out when they see no future and have no hope. If, however, we are working in earnest on a new operating model or a business reinvention, the excitement of what we're doing and where we're going counteracts the stress that precedes burnout. If you're part of a company that claims to be reengineered, but in fact has only downsized in such a way that now half the number of people are doing twice the amount of work, that's a cause for burnout and discouragement.

On the other hand, when people have a clear vision, when they start to experience the productivity of the new work and develop a sense that what they do really matters, then there's a palpable excitement. Even though they may be working longer than ever before, the pleasure in the work offsets the risks and the potential burnout. And this is one of the great rewards of reengineering: Instead of finding people flickering out like old candles, you have a chance to light fires of hope and inspiration, enabling people to see their way along a journey in which they will discover what they do best and how to develop a greater sense of pride and purpose in their work.

CHAPTER 1

MANAGEMENT? WHY REENGINEER MANAGEMENT?

The results are in: Reengineering works—up to a point.
The obstacle is management.
The only way we're going to deliver on the full promise of
reengineering is to start reengineering management—by
reengineering ourselves.

Reengineering is in trouble. It's not easy for me to make this admission. I was one of the two people who introduced the concept.

Reengineering the Corporation has sold nearly two million copies worldwide since it was published in 1993, an astonishing success for a business book. But it's *your* bottom line, not ours, that ought to measure the success of any set of management ideas. And by that measure, there's much more reengineering to do.

Reengineering the Corporation was written to improve business performance by showing managers how to revolutionize their key operational processes—product development, for example, or order fulfillment. And it has worked. I have the evidence of my own eyes and ears, from visits to scores of companies that practice reengineering. I have the testimony of more than 150 managers, gathered over 18 months' worth of interviews for this book. I have the evidence, too, of the first thorough study of the effects of the would-be revolution.

That study, "The State of Reengineering Report," was conducted in early 1994 by CSC Index, the strategic management consulting arm of the firm I head. Six hundred and twenty-one companies, representing a sample of 6,000 of the largest corporations in North America and Europe, completed an extensive questionnaire. The sample showed that fully 69 percent of the 497 American companies responding, and 75 percent of the 124 European, were already engaged in one or more reengineering projects, and that half of the remaining companies were thinking about such projects.

In North America, projects tended to be driven by competition and customer pressure, and focused therefore on processes with direct customer contact—e.g., customer service (25 percent), order fulfillment (16 percent), and customer acquisition (11 percent). In Europe, the focus was on cost-cutting initiatives in manufacturing and its service-industry equivalents (23 percent). On both continents there were a smattering of projects across the full range of operational processes: 9 percent on links in the inbound supply chain, 6 percent on corporate information systems, 4 percent on product development, and so on.

Many companies reported big changes and reaped big rewards. An American mining company, for example, saw its revenues increase by 30 percent and its market share by 20 percent, while its costs went down 12 percent and its cycle time 25 percent. A European retail group gained a 50 percent improvement in cycle time and a 15 percent improvement in productivity. After reengineering its inventory-replenishment process, a U.S. clothing manufacturer doubled sales, increased its market share by 50 percent, and cut its cycle time by 25 percent. A North American chemical company cut its order-delivery time by more than 50 percent and its costs by more than $300 million.

There have been many equally dramatic success stories. On the whole, however, even substantial reengineering payoffs appear to have fallen well short of their potential. *Reengineering the Corporation* set big goals: 70 percent decreases in cycle time and 40 percent decreases in costs; 40 percent increases in customer satisfaction, quality, and revenue; and 25 percent growth in market share. Although the jury is still out on 71 percent of the ongoing North American reengineering efforts in our sample, overall, the study shows, participants failed to attain these benchmarks by as much as 30 percent.

This partial revolution is not the one I intended. If I've learned anything in the last 18 months, it is that the revolution we started has gone, at best, only halfway. I have also learned that half a revolution is not better than none. It may, in fact, be worse.

Our earlier book was largely about reengineering *work*—the operational processes performed by salespeople, clerks, factory and warehouse hands, repair people, engineers, technicians, customer-service folks, field representatives—anyone and everyone in the value-adding chain. Now, in this book, I must shift my focus. This book is not about operational processes. It is about managing, written for managers, and (it may be reassuring to note) by a manager. It is about *us*, about changing our managerial work, the way we think about, organize, inspire, deploy, enable, measure, and reward the value-adding operational work. It is about changing management itself.

But who, exactly, is a manager these days? How do we know one when we see one?

In the wholeheartedly reengineered corporation, responsibility and authority are so widely distributed throughout the organization that virtually everyone becomes a manager, if only of his or her own work. Still, there's no ignoring two facts. First, as our study shows, the thoroughly reengineered corporation is as yet a rarity. Second, even a reengineering revolution leaves some people with more general authority and responsibility than it leaves others. The old pyramid may be flattened out, but the remnants are still discernible in these levels of managerial accountability:

- Self-managers—people who may not think of themselves as managers because, in the last analysis, they answer only for the quality of their own work. Examples include customer-service representatives, researchers, salespeople, lawyers, and accountants—in short, just about everyone working individually or as a member of a team.
- Process and people managers—those who answer for the work of others, usually individuals, a team, or group of teams working closely with customers or on a specific process. An example would be a manager of a case team, a group of people who have among them all the skills needed to handle a specific process—the installation of a telephone, say, or the sale of an insurance policy, or the development of a new drug. In the reengineered workplace, employees often rotate in and out of this sort of managerial responsibility as the occasion demands.
- Expertise managers—people whose responsibility is the care and development of a company's intelligence (in all senses of the word). Examples are technology managers and managers of human resource development programs.
- Enterprise managers—CEOs, division heads, all those with profit-and-loss responsibility. "Senior management" we used to call them, when business authority was established by years of service.

This book is written for managers on all these levels. It is written out of the conviction, buttressed by solid evidence, that without their help the revolution we began with the 1993 book will remain painfully incomplete. We certainly knew back then that management was critical to reengineering's success. But not until we had some real experience of how these ideas worked in practice did we begin to understand how radically managers themselves would have to change their way of doing things for

reengineering to fulfill its promise. Anything less than a fundamental revolution in actual management *practice*, we discovered,
is like a communist regime introducing free enterprise into a
controlled economy while trying to hold on to power. It can be
done for a while (look at China), but no one supposes that such
an arrangement can last. Something's gotta give, and history
shows that it's not going to be free enterprise. It has to be management. If management doesn't change, reengineering will be
stopped in its tracks, and we can't afford to let that happen.

Look what takes place when work gets reengineered and
management doesn't:

- The three vice presidents (for sales, service, and order-
fulfillment) at a major computer company were thrilled that
reengineered work processes promised to cut product introduc-
tion time in half, raise customer retention rates by 20 percent,
and slice 30 percent from administrative costs in their areas.
They weren't thrilled enough, however, to willingly give up control of their fiefdoms and collaborate. Result: The reengineering
effort died a year after its inception.

- A large European aerospace company, acknowledging that
it was in trouble, encouraged the launch of multiple reengineering efforts. Redesign teams were authorized and fundamental
changes to operations were proposed. Presentations were made
to senior management, but no action was taken. Management
was unable to move, frozen by the question of the company's
future. Everything stopped. Result: demoralized workers. The
best prospect for the company: acquisition.

- A large pharmaceutical company saw its customers growing more and more annoyed at having to deal with each of its
business units separately. The reengineering solution was to inte-
grate the sales and distribution operations of all the units. The
unit heads protested, arguing that they had to retain control of
these functions. The CEO and chairman refused to act on the
necessary changes, afraid of reform's inevitable disruption. Busi-

ness was good before the current recession, they argued, and would rebound when it was over. Result: For this company, the recession goes on and on.

• Old management practices subverted an insurance company's ambitious reengineering effort to introduce teams to the process of new customer acquisition. The rub came with the news that team members would evaluate each others' performances. Such measures "never work," declared the human resources chief, adding that performances could be evaluated only by an "objective observer"—to wit, a manager. Result: end of teams, end of reengineering.

• And there are other strange phenomena I am observing broadly across many companies that are reengineering: Senior managers are angrily complaining that middle managers are entrenched, blocking the necessary changes; middle managers are bitterly complaining that senior managers have neither the vision nor fortitude to take the enterprise through the changes. As you already know, there may be some truth in both accusations.

"Reengineering" has proved to be an extraordinarily popular concept. The trouble is, popular concepts sometimes look like magic, and the more popular they become, the more powerful the magic seems. Some managers, misled by wishful thinking, believe that merely repeating the key words in *Reengineering the Corporation* is enough to bring the transformation, like the newsboy in the comic strip who yelled "Shazaam!" and became powerful Captain Marvel. Managers have been saying, "Fundamental!" "Dramatic!" "Radical!" "Processes!"—and, lo, that which they proclaim to be so *is* so . . . they hope.

Unfortunately, nothing is that simple. Reengineering prescribes *actions*, not words, and difficult, long-term actions at that, not just one-shot expedients like downsizing or outsourcing. Reengineering involves a voyage that will last years, possibly our entire management lifetime.

For us managers, nothing seems sure anymore, neither our professional know-how nor our career paths—and certainly not our job security. For failed CEOs, the consequences are partially mitigated by gold and platinum parachutes, but the parachutes themselves are a measure, by way of compensation, of the exponential increase in the pressures on top corporate officers. Management has joined the ranks of the dangerous professions.

I shall spell all this out in the pages that follow, a practical exploration of the key questions that the actual practice of reengineering (successful and otherwise) has kicked up, all of which must be addressed for reengineering to succeed. There are four broad issues:

- *Issues of purpose.* Insistently, persistently, relentlessly, the new manager must ask, "What for?" What is it that we're in business for? What is this process for? This product? This task? This team? This job? What are we doing here, anyway?

- *Issues of culture.* If successful reengineering requires a change in a company's whole culture, as seems to be the case in many instances, how is it to be accomplished by the same management that did so well in the old culture? If it is true (and it is) that reengineering is unlikely to succeed where the corporate atmosphere is charged with fear (and its twin, mistrust), how do we generate another, better environment—one, say, of willingness and mutual confidence?

- *Issues of process and performance.* How do we get the kind of processes we want? How do we get the performances we need from our people? How do we set norms and standards, or measure results—for worker performance, management performance, and the performance of the whole enterprise? Reengineering usually demands radical objectives, leadership, and political skills to realize. But how do we know whether we have the stuff? What does it take to be a good manager today?

- *Issues of people.* Who do we want to work with? How can we find them from both inside and outside the company? How do we get them to want to work with us? How do we know whether they're the kind of people we want?

Although these are hard questions to pose, they are harder to answer—and learning to live the answer is far harder still. As I look at the practice of business management today, I sometimes think of the exchange between Vladimir and Estragon in Beckett's *Waiting for Godot*. The two wretches have been shuffling along in silence, when suddenly Estragon groans, "I can't stand it anymore." To which Vladimir says, "Oh, yes, you can."

Fortunately, things are not as bad as that. For most of us, "Yes, you can" is not yet a curse. It is an opportunity for us to reinvent ourselves.

We must look to ourselves, and to each other, to find the personal resources we need to do our jobs—the courage and trust and smarts. That's where this book, I hope, can be especially useful. I can provide some ideas, even some encouragement. But managers cannot hope to carry out their responsibilities to employees and investors without first facing up to the tensions, problems, and conflicts of corporate leadership today.

This book is for people I know as heroes and heroines. They are the protagonists in the great central drama of our time—the creation of a better workplace and the production of wealth. But never before has this drama been so shot through with peril, conflict, and anxiety. Never before has it been so heightened by raw contingency. And never before have its opportunities—personal and corporate—been so vast, or so potentially rewarding. This book is for those who, in the face of these realities, are keen for the battle and determined to win.

CHAPTER 2

THE ORDEAL OF MANAGEMENT

We must dramatically improve business results, now, and do
it while earning the hearts and minds of our people.
To make things still more difficult, "now" has no traditions,
no precedents, no time-tested formulas.
Now has never been seen before.

Nothing is simple anymore. Nothing is stable. The business environment is changing before our eyes, rapidly, radically, perplexingly.

Now, whatever we do is not enough. Incremental change is what we're used to: the kind we could manage gradually, with careful planning, broad consensus-building, and controlled execution. Now we must not only manage change, we must create change—big change—and fast. If we stop for a leisurely consideration of the issues, the situation will alter in front of our eyes and our careful judgments will not apply.

Everything is in question. The old ways of managing no longer work. The organization charts, the compensation schemes, the hierarchies, the vertical organization, the whole tool kit of command-and-control management techniques no longer work.

Everyone must change. The change will go deeper than technique. It touches not merely what managers do, but who they are. Not just their sense of the task, but their sense of themselves. Not just what they know, but how they think. Not just their way of seeing the world, but their way of living in the world.

These refrains will keep coming at you in this book. *Nothing is simple. Whatever you do is not enough. Everything is in question. Everyone must change.*

Consider the news from Saturn—the General Motors division, not the planet. On August 2, 1991, at the end of Saturn's first year of production, Alan G. Perriton, Saturn's director of materials management, gave a speech in the heart of Old Motor City: Traverse City, Michigan. You could practically hear the trumpets sounding—for Saturn, for GM, for America!

> Surveys show that, in new car sales per outlet, Saturn is matching or exceeding Honda, and clearly exceeding Toyota. . . .
>
> Ninety-eight percent [of our customers] would enthusiastically recommend their Saturn car to a friend, neighbor or relative. And they're equally excited by the purchase experience. . . .
>
> J. D. Power's initial quality survey sends Saturn home with the gold medal.
>
> I'm here to tell you that Saturn has scored a word-of-mouth home run.

Now it is two and a half years later, and Saturn still makes a top-quality car; still has a cult following in a highly desirable demographic (college-educated baby boomers); still has the avant-garde, just-in-time production system and the no-hassle, courteous sales-and-service system that were the envy of managers in all the other GM divisions; still has the union deal that allows those systems—*and still* is making a very marginal profit.

"Saturn, GM's Big Hope, Is Taking Its First Lumps," said the *New York Times* in its March 1994 front-page story. Inside the paper, we learn what the stock analysts are saying, what the union guys are saying, and rumors of what GM's new leadership is saying. What they're saying is not good. Saturn may have changed the way cars are made, sold, and serviced, all for the better, but the "better" has not yet been good enough. The bottom line is still barely black and recalls have tarnished the car's quality image.

And do you want to know the worst of it? The *Times* didn't mention the fact, but Saturn started with the same inestimable advantage that the Germans and the Japanese had after World War II. It started with a clean slate—and even that wasn't enough.

How far a company must go to succeed shouldn't come as a surprise. In 1993, Michael Hammer and I wrote in *Reengineering the Corporation*, "A set of principles laid down more than two centuries ago has shaped . . . American businesses throughout [this century]. . . . The time has come to retire those principles and adopt a new set. The alternative is for corporate America to close its doors and go out of business. The choice is that . . . stark."

Peter Drucker has put it just as bluntly: "Every organization has to prepare for the abandonment of everything it does."

But what is this "everything" that we must abandon? And why must we abandon it? To answer that question, we must look for a moment at how our "modern day" managerial thinking was shaped.

THE METAPHOR OF THE CORPORATE MACHINE

"A great business," said Henry Ford, who knew one when he saw one, "is really too big to be human." The pronouncement, which many people would agree with, begs an interesting question: If a great business can't be human, what can it be? Some image, or metaphor, is called for. Our whole *sense* of a business depends on it, as does our image of the people who work there, of what we can ask of them, of ourselves as managers, and of our work.

People like to think that businesses are built of numbers (as in "the bottom line"), or forces (as in "market forces"), or power (as in "the power of the CEO"), or things ("the product"), or even flesh and blood ("our people"). But this is wrong. In the first instance, and most subsequent instances, businesses are made of ideas—ideas expressed as words. And there's not much question what word Ford would have chosen to describe his "great business." He would have called it a *machine*.

This fateful figure of speech has been around for a long time. The Greeks had the notion that the human brain behaved like a catapult. Water mills were a favorite image until the seventeenth century, at which point Isaac Newton's discoveries made people think of clocks. Then the steam engine came along, then the electric generator, then the internal combustion engine, whereupon we had the organization that ran like a "well-oiled" machine. Nowadays, of course, we have the computer, with its software, which many people believe not only models the human brain, but *is* a human brain. Henry Ford, to judge from the vast museum of machinery he founded in Dearborn, Michigan, might have had in mind anything from a toaster to an airplane—although, his own favorite machines, of course, were the assembly line and the Model T.

Alfred P. Sloan, Jr., the business genius who shaped the General Motors we know today, was the other great car man of the early twentieth century. And it's safe to say that he, too, thought of a great business in terms of the machine metaphor. Sloan's ideas, like those of many managers of his generation, were influenced by Frederick S. Taylor, a proper Philadelphian who became a pioneer in the study of work. Taylor taught that there was one optimal way to accomplish every industrial task, and one method of discovering that way. You had only to subject the task to a time-and-motion analysis, breaking it down into discrete actions performed over specified lengths of time. Then you trained your workers to perform according to the norms established by the analysis.

A famous photograph of the 1940s tells where this led. A

man who tightened bolts on an assembly line for 20 years has a right arm like Popeye's; the left is normal. The meaning is all too clear. The man has become part of the assembly-line machine.

But if we hold the focus on Popeye we will miss Sloan's most important contribution. Through Sloan, the influence of Taylor's ideas went well beyond the mechanization of human *labor*, to the mechanization of management. Sloan imagined, and in fact realized, a *management machine*, a way to build not just cars, but an entire company. Although Sloan wanted GM to be "decentralized," as he says in his autobiography, he also wanted to run it on "a principle of coordination"—the principle, it turned out, of central command-and-control. His words betray him. He believed that he had created something new, the "objective organization," as distinct from one that was dependent on the "subjectivity of personalities." But there is only one thing in the world that is both productive and nonsubjective. It isn't a human being, or even an organization of human beings. It is a machine.

Don't dismiss this notion too fast. It had, and continues to have, tremendous appeal to all of us. Why? Because it is an *ideal*, a vision of perfected human activity. Human beings are just fine; we wouldn't be anything else. But we are undependable: We get distracted, tired, angry, lusty, and ornery. We get depressed, we're drawn this way and that, grumbling about doing what's good for us. We scheme and battle. Organizational machines, or so the metaphor wants us to believe, do not suffer from any of these disabilities. Organizational machines normally rely on humans only at the most elementary level of their being, for raw energy that courses through the mechanism once it's been built and started, like steam, diesel fuel, or electricity through a great ship. These machines are basically organization charts brought to life in work slots and duty stations, all held together by "chains" of command and "lines" of authority. The more refined human qualities—imagination, say, or judgment, decisiveness, or adaptability—have their time and place in these structures. But the time is at the beginning of the enterprise, when the ship must be designed and constructed. And the place is at the top—on the bridge. Thereafter, with careful command

and control, sound navigation and maintenance, the ship should operate with perfect reliability and rationality (no "subjectivity," no "politics"). Sloan didn't depend on "car men" to obey his orders at the levers and buttons of GM. Instead, he chose "money men," manipulators and guardians of the one true universal, all-purpose instrument in the human tool kit—capital.

There's an additional appeal to the machine metaphor. It graphically rationalizes the major concerns of an earlier era's top (and wanna-be top) managers—concerns for efficiency, professionalism, power, and prestige. In short, the metaphor lies close to the heart of a managerial ideology. This is not to put it down. Like all ideologies, this one could never have survived without a heady mixture of reason and idealism. Nor could it have survived unless it met the needs and wants of the society that gave it birth. And this one did—as a model, the corporate "machine" was triumphant for 25 years.

THE ERA OF SMOOTH SAILING

If it was ever plausible to speak of an "American Century," in Henry Luce's proud phrase, it was during the quarter century after the defeat of Germany and Japan. No news from Saturn disturbed those years, just success after success. For those two-and-a-half decades, the Era of Smooth Sailing, as I think of it, the laurels belonged to America's top business managers, the captains of our ships of productivity.

The last time we managers had looked so good was at the very beginning of the so-called Managerial Revolution. That was back around 1917, when the children and grandchildren of the great industry-builders of the nineteenth century handed over command of the businesses and capital they had inherited to a new breed of professional managers, like Sloan. But then came the Great Depression and the somewhat unfair humiliation of the professional managers' hero-president, Herbert Hoover. Management then lost a notch or two in the status stakes.

Our prestige began to revive during World War II, but our glory years were unquestionably bounded by those two forgettable dates—1948 to 1973. Never in history had a whole people flourished as we Americans did in those years—in education, affluence, and quality of life. From boardroom to executive suite, from salesroom to factory floor, from suburban split-level to exurban estate, it was morning in America, the dawn of a glorious day when everything seemed possible.

What had occurred in America was an astonishing democratization, not just of opportunity, but of a *sense* of opportunity. All Americans, with the shameful exception of some minority groups, now believed that they inherited a full deck of life's chances merely by being born American. *Everyone*, not just owners and managers, now believed in a great new secular faith of growth. And growth was not just economic, but personal, cultural, and spiritual as well.

At the same time, many Americans, business executives foremost among them, began to see the world in a new way—as an extension of America's internal market. American corporations and financial services, and the American dollar, dominated world trade as no country or currency had since Britain and the pound in the nineteenth century. J. J. Servan-Schreiber's famous book *The American Challenge*, published in 1967, went so far as to predict that European nations would become industrial satellites of the United States.

All this was a stupendous achievement for our society. Growth seemed to fulfill the promise of America; it looked effortless and endless. And much of the credit for shaping the workplace and creating the wealth that made it possible went to us business managers. On the basis of the growth rate established in the Smooth Sailing years, for example, the average American family could look backward to a doubling of family income in one generation; and it could look forward to at least the same in each future generation.

POWER SHIFT: THE CAPTAINS' NEW CAPTAINS

Today, of course, we know that that growth was finite. Today, as current rates of productivity increase, the average American family can expect its descendants to double the current family income in about four centuries, or 16 generations. As a result, there's a new mood of loss and betrayal in our country these days, summed up by a bitter new article of faith: *For the first time in our history a generation of Americans is going to have a lower standard of living than its parents.*

For managers, this blow to the American Dream simply adds historical urgency to our age-old challenge—to go on shaping the workplaces and creating the wealth to improve the quality of human life and work. If we can claim much of the responsibility for the economic triumphs of 1948 to 1973, a period that began with its own difficulties, then we can't very well duck responsibility for taking on the grave problems we face at the beginning of the current era.

But what are those problems? Where do they come from? What on earth happened in 1973?

Well, it was around 1973 that oil prices shot up, Watergate hit the headlines, and Vietnam was finally perceived to be a lost cause. The idealism of the 1960s was going flat, and the conservatism of the 1950s was going sour. Meanwhile, all the indices of growth were going down, while inflation was going up, up, up. For us managers, specifically, the new era amounted to a change of climate: No more smooth sailing, only year after year of rough weather.

The root causes of this change remain controversial, but most fingers point to a fundamental power shift affecting virtually every business anywhere. The professional managers, like Alfred Sloan, who took command of the corporate economy around World War I, were losing control of their "machines." Power for some years now had been flowing outward toward customers and investors, the "elements," the winds and the waves, in which businesses must make their way. Three forces caused the power shift. First, the achievements of the Smooth Sailing years put money in people's pockets and investment accounts—especially American pockets and accounts—as never before in history. This great attraction encouraged companies and governments all over the world to organize themselves to produce goods and services for sale in America, then in Europe, then wherever there was money to buy them. The second force was postwar America's magnificently self-confident openness to free trade, and its insistence on imposing free-trade policies on the world. Third was the so-called Digital Revolution in communications technology, which enabled capital and information (information about the ROI of capital, for one thing; information about the relative values of products and services, for another) to fly around the globe at the speed of light.

And so were born the "global economy" and "global competition," the phrases we use to describe what is essentially a fully liberated and empowered market of moneyed customers, with an entourage of rival businesses struggling for their favor, and colossal pools of capital betting on hopeful winners of the struggle.

From the manager's point of view, whether customers or investors ended up with more power is a good question. Growing wealth and declining restraints ("protection") on trade endow both of them with a fantastical new range of choices (and opportunities to change their choices) among products and investments. Still, as far as managers are concerned, the most powerful of the new bosses are undoubtedly the customers. For if managers can win them, they won't have much trouble winning investors.

This is not altogether good news. Winning customers has never been harder. Today's customers, as *Fortune* put it, are "the sharpest, most-educated customers [that] marketers have ever faced." In today's marketplaces, it's no longer a question of *caveat emptor*, but of *caveat factor*. Customers today are characterized by their relentless demands in quality, service, and price; by their willingness to act on a default of contract; by their disloyalty. All this puts them as far away from the gentle, grateful, loyal customers of the 1950s and 1960s as a pirate crew is from a platoon of crew-cut Marines.

Look at the range of choices customers are being offered today. Sony turns out four new products a day, and a new Walkman model every three weeks. In 1991, 64 new varieties of spaghetti sauce appeared on the market. In 1992 alone Heinz introduced more than 500 new products worldwide. Rubbermaid turns out an average of one new product a day. The first laundry detergent, Tide, was introduced by Procter & Gamble in 1946. For 38 years, it ruled its market alone. Then, feeling the heat of a fickle public, P&G felt the need to add Unscented Tide and Liquid Tide (1984), Tide with bleach (1988), concentrated Ultra Tide (1990), and Tide with bleach alternative (1992). And so it goes virtually everywhere, from big-ticket items like computers to everyday items like laundry soap.

In fact, the new power and freedom of the customer has destroyed all the fond managerial assumptions of the Smooth Sailing years. No more unearned, inherited brand loyalties ("Our family always buys Fords"); no more cordial complicity among rivals in the same markets; no more confident pass-alongs of rising wages and benefits in the form of higher prices; no more easy reliance on high entry costs to keep out upstart competitors; and no more indulgent protection by national governments.

The last is a key point. There's hardly a government left in the world, whether communist, socialist, or free-market conservative, that isn't openly or wishfully committed to a policy of "tough love" toward its business sector. The "love" is for business as benefactor: Governments now realize that business, and only business, can provide the jobs that provide the paychecks that provide government with the two things it needs to keep going—the tax money that pays for services, and a sense of prosperity that translates as votes. The "toughness" is for business as beseecher: Governments, with a few exceptions, now realize that protecting business enterprises creates bloated companies unable to compete in global markets. In local markets it is like taking money (in higher prices and reduced choices) from consumers—a.k.a. voters. At the end of the day, governmental tough love speaks to the problems of business managers with a remarkably coherent message, "Sure, things are rough out there. We can't help that. In fact, for the consumers' sake, fight it out. But there's also lots of money to be made. Get your share. You're on your own. May the best man or woman win!"

Actually, governments know that the best man and woman— the consumer-voter—has already won. And this means managers will never be able to relax again. Neither government nor the customer will let them.

THE WRECK OF THE MACHINE

Whatever name we give to this new regime—*a dictatorship of the customariat* or (as I prefer to see it) *a market democracy*—it's causing a total revolution within the traditional, machine-like corporation. The corporate ship is becoming a vessel the likes of which no one has ever seen before.

Be prepared to abandon everything, says Peter Drucker, lest we have to abandon the ship. But to many managers it seems that the first thing to be thrown overboard is ourselves. Everyone knows the figures. The human jetsam of the last five years adds up to 1.4 million executives, managers, and administrative professionals, as against 782,000 from 1981 to 1986. The figure (which counts neither the vast numbers of more-or-less obligatory early retirements, nor the "opportunity losses" of hundreds of thousands of jobs struck off the nation's organization charts) amounts to 23,000 managerial jobs a month, 133 every working hour. That number may not come as a surprise. If you haven't experienced management attrition in your own company yet, you have certainly read about it daily on the business pages of your newspaper. The first wave of managerial exodus came purely from the need to reduce costs in order for companies to remain competitive—for some, to remain in business. The second wave came with a challenge that some managers didn't add any business value. It's almost become the fashion to close "headquarters," a sign of the "lean and mean" image to which some companies aspire. The third wave came with a little more forethought, a recognition that many managers—especially middle managers—principally gathered and moved information through a bureaucracy and that information technology had finally obviated their need. And then came reengineering, with managerial accountability being pushed down and out as work becomes more self-managed, and the need for many of the managers in our organizations being challenged.

Now all of these actions were arguably options that senior management chose to exercise—sometimes with little other choice. Still, managers up to now may have felt in control. But no one will be insulated from the next wave: the collapse of the old corporate machine. The ferocious, unrelenting competition for the customer's approval has been straining every work process in almost every company in the world, from product development to customer service. *Reengineering the Corporation* was a highly successful book because it came on the market at just the right time—to meet an urgent, not to say frantic, need to reinvent these processes.

But now, as we saw all too clearly in Chapter 1, the equally urgent need is to reinvent the processes of management, to bend them to the new realities of the demands of the marketplace. As Shirley Richard, a "reengineer" at Arizona Public Service, told us in an interview, the greatest drawback of the old "machine" metaphor was that it fostered a culture of bureaucracy—that is, a moral environment that focuses on "activity, not results." Thus, as customers make tougher and tougher demands on a company's services and products, those rational "machines" have been groaning and popping in protest at the pressure.

And it's specifically the "chains" of command, the "lines" of authority, the very stuff that held Sloan's automaton together, that are groaning and popping the loudest. For what's happening is an *internal power shift* to match the external one from management out to the free markets. Customers, flexing their new muscle, are growing ever more exacting, even (or so it seems to the old captains) uppity. And how do they express their power? *They're always asking to speak to the person in charge!*

But who *is* in charge? As reengineers see it, this question is the beginning of wisdom. The customer doesn't really want to speak to the traditional "person in charge." Such a person, if he or she exists, is just a name in a box on the organizational chart, and what the customer wants, the name-in-a-box probably can't give him. The customer wants help, service, a product, or a solution to a problem. He doesn't want someone whose only possible role in the affair might be to tell someone else to give him what he wants. So, say the reengineers, let's redesign our processes so that customers can talk with someone who can do something that will actually help them—that should be the real person in charge.

And with that neat, logical, and altogether drastic redesign, the whole of Mr. Sloan's wonderfully rational machine falls apart. For to say that the person in charge is the person who can help the customer (and vice versa) is to make entire layers and branches of the old organization chart "redundant," as our British friends say. All those boxes are suddenly revealed to be meaningless, and their inhabitants irrelevant. Why? Because their meaning and power, such as they were, were always *internal*; that is, wholly concerned with the functioning of the machine itself. The great corporate vessels of the Sloan sort were really cruise ships: huge facilities for the enjoyment of passengers, yes; majestic powers of command and control for their top officers, yes; but for all the other officers on board, not much more than a floating system of rewards, promotions, and privileges—in a phrase, a self-serving bureaucracy.

In the new climate, with competitive ships constantly looming up over the horizon, with top officers preoccupied by constant problems of navigation and lousy weather, with passengers constantly ready to revolt and jump ship, and with the crew totally absorbed in trying to make the passengers happy, the junior officers may even ask themselves, "What the heck are we doing here?"

It's a good question (and one for which I'll give answers later in this book). But the point I want to make here concerns the question with which I began this chapter: What is the "everything" that Peter Drucker says we must be prepared to abandon?

It is not the ship, we may hope. Nor is it jobs. Jobs are being lost, and will continue to be lost for some time. Reengineering will teach us to do far more with much less. But eventually reengineering should bring about such a tight fit between market opportunities and corporate abilities that jobs will be created. For some period, downsizing and outsourcing will be byproducts of reengineering, no doubt about it, but they are not by any means the thing itself, nor one of its purposes.

No, in the last analysis, what must be abandoned by the new management of our corporate ships—that is, both officers *and* crew—is a whole ideology, a whole way of thinking about power. Power no longer belongs in boxes, in titles, in ranks. In the new heavy weather, those are nothing more than heady abstractions, eloquent vacancies, and they count for nothing. What counts—for power, authority, responsibility—is what you can do, you yourself, you with your own skills and personal qualities.

At the deepest level, then, the ordeal of management is revealing something about a great change not only in business organizations, but in the larger society. The democracy of customers, voting with their money, is summoning a meritocracy of people and producers, responding with everything they've got.

CHAPTER 3

LIVING THE QUESTIONS

Questions for the middle of the day.
And the middle of the night.
How can I do this faster? How can I do it for less?
What if I don't do it at all?
Are all successful companies doomed to extinction?
What is this work for? What are we aiming at here?
What is the market? Who is the customer?
How can we work better, and better, and better?

For Rick Zaffarano, the test of his faith came way too soon—his faith, that is, in his fellow associates, and in reengineering. Zaffarano is a young, articulate manager at Hannaford Brothers, the supermarket-chain operators based in Portland, Maine. In 1993, he was assigned the job of organizing a new warehouse operation in New York State. This he did, pushing authority, responsibility, and team self-management as far as he thought they could go. And perhaps (how could he tell?) farther.

The test came early on. A truck tipped over in a winter storm, and its cargo was destroyed. Zaffarano knew that the store to which the truck was going would run short if they didn't get a new shipment on the way. Everyone else in the warehouse knew it, too. I'll let Zaffarano tell the rest of the story as he told it to us; the fears and the mistrust were his, after all:

> It was the end of the day, and everybody was tired and anxious to go home. I couldn't just go and order people to stay, as I might have in the old days. I had to talk to the team coordinators—not management types, mind you, but associates picked by the teams themselves.
>
> I told them, one by one, what I wanted to get done and that I didn't want to wait until the next day. There was disagreement— some of the guys thought I was asking too much. So I suggested that we pull the whole group together and try to work out a scenario. I said I'd live with their decision, whatever it was.
>
> I have to say, I had a few bad minutes after I took that risk. I knew that if they decided to go home, I was going to be in a real bind. In the end, remember, I was going to have to answer for what happened that night. On the other hand, I wanted to prove that intelligent people who care about the job will make the right decision when given the right information.
>
> And I won my bet. The group said, "Hey, we have to do it, so let's do it." Later on one of the coordinators said to me, "I guess I didn't think the guys would vote that way." I appreciated his frankness. My gamble paid off, I think, largely because I offered to live with their decision.

In the months since that night, Zaffarano has had plenty of time to reflect on what it meant to him. "Did you know that there are times when a manager can feel *dis*empowered?" he said. Many times, in many subsequent crunches like the one involving the capsized truck, he has felt the whole nine yards of fear that reengineering often brings to managers. There's the fear of letting go, the fear of losing control, the fear of misplaced trust, of betrayal, the fear of losing popularity (or of not being thought "tough"), and always, of course, the fear of failure. Here's Zaffarano again:

I may know from past experience in other warehouses what needs to be done, and there's a terrific temptation to just go ahead and *order* it. But the real trick is not to command, not to manipulate, but to share information and educate. That's what all the talk about "empowerment" really comes down to, isn't it? To help people rise to a level of maturity where they will make the right and reasonable decision.

Which isn't to say that they always do, or always will. Still, when a team makes a poor decision, we'll stand aside and let them stub their toe. Sometimes, if we honestly feel that they're going to break a *leg*, say, or the company's leg, then we'll intervene. We've done that a couple of times, but really, you know, it's not a good idea. The best thing is, you let the team know that you understand their viewpoint, but that all your business experience tells you that the thing has to be done differently; then you stand aside.

There are many managers like Rick Zaffarano, I've found. But there are many more I've found who don't even come close to governing their fears of the reengineered workplace as well as he does. For example, I remember talking management talk recently with the editor of a major national magazine. We were talking theoretically, but when I asked him a few delicate questions about the processes at his own shop—copy-editing and research, for example: why they couldn't be done more efficiently by freelancers plugged into the main office by modem— he grew very agitated. Impossible, he exclaimed, I need these people to be near me at all times . . . how can they possibly know what to do unless they can talk to me . . . a magazine is a *community* . . . you can't farm out a community . . . and so on. I quickly changed the subject.

"The biggest complaint [about reengineering] we heard again and again from managers concerned their lack of control," Debra Smithart, executive vice president and CFO of the restaurant-chain company Brinker International, told us in an interview. "'What is going to happen if we aren't controlling things?'—that's what some department heads always wanted to know. What they really were afraid of is that they wouldn't be important."

Loss of (self) importance undoubtedly is a fear of some managers who are caught up in a reengineering project, but not many. The prospect of losing control taps into a far more basic anxiety than the prospect of losing status. For most of us, status issues are in the serious-but-not-grave category. Control issues, however, go back to infancy, when they seemed like (and sometimes were) matters of life or death. That's surely why, in our interviews for this book, the most vivid moments always came when we touched the "control" button. Debra Smithart herself, for instance, admitted, "I've wanted to strangle about half my staff on occasion." Roger Easom, manager of FedEx's Management Education program, addressed the issue with biting humor: "I suppose at some point in every manager's career, on one of those days when nothing seems to go right, we've all had the thought, 'Why can't people be more like cattle?'" Even Rick Zaffarano, who's as enthusiastic and intelligent a proponent of reengineering as we've met, acknowledges:

> The hard part is having to share power. No matter how you cut it, after a while you want to just make your own decision and follow it through. I confess that my own thinking tends to be hierarchical in certain situations. . . . I like to be able to say yes or no without having to confer all the time and seek consensus. So there are some drawbacks for me in the new order, but I realize it's the right thing to do.

We're going to dig deeper in this chapter than the fear of letting go of command-and-control, however. And as we do, we'll find a whole pattern of thought, a whole mentality, a whole set of ideals and expectations. It's very hard indeed, but these, too, must be let go:

• We have to leave behind *perfectionist* organizational thinking, with its faith in an eternal, universally right way of doing things. Instead, our thinking must be radically *experimental*. If we don't like it, too bad; we have no choice. As PepsiCo's Wayne Calloway says, "The marketplace just won't let you stand still."

• We have to abandon the management credo "*Get it right, then keep it going*" and embrace the credo "*Get it right and make it better, and better, and better,*" or even "*Make it something else.*" We must give up the comforting illusion that there is one conclusive solution to any business (or human) problem, and live with the fact that each problem changes virtually overnight, and no two problems are exactly the same, that many problems can only be coped with. As Ralph E. Spurgin, president of Limited Credit Services, a division of The Limited, Inc., puts it: "Think about what you're doing, so that you're constantly asking: How can I do this better? How can I do it for less? What if I don't do it at all?"

• We have to let go of any feeling of despair about people, the despair underlying the fantasy of the perfect organization. It's easy to sometimes feel that we human beings are essentially unreliable and limited and therefore must be forced to do our duty by chains of command, compartments of function, and lines of authority. But instead we must hold fast to our *faith* in human beings: the knowledge and belief that we are all eager to learn, and capable of dedication, high spirits, and individual responsibility. Ann Monroe, of Blue Cross of California, described this when she told me, "We believe that if people understand what's needed, the effort will follow. This has been proven time and time again—given the tools and the training, they will do the job."

• We have to trade in the airy abstraction of *ex officio authority* for the messier reality of *existential authority*. We must wake up to the fact that authority is no longer vested in a place on the organization chart, but in the ability to do a job better for the customer. "All corporations dream about . . . initiative," Wayne Calloway says, "but they seldom get it. The reason is that too many controls and too much supervision stifle the people on the scene. They feel restricted, intimidated, or bored."

• We have to overthrow the *tyranny of numerical accountancy*, with its insistence that value is in measurable *things*, and that money is the measure of all things. Certainly, everything we do must contribute to our business performance. But the best way to measure the value of those contributions is to submit them to the judgment of *the consumer*, with his many, often conflicting value-demands, not all of them reducible to money-values. Debra Smithart again, telling us what it was like "before": "In our old company everything had to be evaluated on a financial basis. If you couldn't cost justify it, you couldn't do it."

• We must keep our old *adversarial/competitive* strategy of managerial betterment, with its slogan, "May the Best Man (woman, product, company, idea) Win!" But we must keep it in its proper place. We must also learn a *supportive* strategy, with its belief that things get better, too, when people are allowed to make mistakes, to learn from them, and to go on to their "personal best." Leslie H. Wexner, the founder, chairman, and CEO of The Limited, Inc., said, "I want our people to hit home runs, but I remember that when Babe Ruth was the home run king, he also led the league in strikeouts."

• We must broaden our age-old devotion to *growth* to include an equally old but only recently rediscovered devotion to *service*. In other words, "More is always better" must give way to "Better is always better—for the customer and us." Reaching "better" can sometimes be measured in numbers, but at other times "better" will remain abstract. As Masaru Ibuka, founder and honorary chairman of Sony Corp., puts it, "There is a spiritual side of the world that is very unpredictable and vague, that is the source of human creativity."

• We have to jettison our *monistic* way of thinking and get used to a *pluralistic* way of thinking. That is, we must see people (including ourselves) not as having *a* skill, but as being *many-sided*, as potentially *multi-skilled*. We must switch from thinking of *one-function departments* to thinking of *polyvalent teams*. The *one-goal enterprise* must become the *all-goal enterprise*. We must stop orienting ourselves in terms of a *single-center, single-*

peak organization, and start orienting ourselves in terms of a *polycentric* or *federal* organization.

• We must abandon thoughts of corporate *discipline*, and focus on corporate spirit. That is, we must discard the fantasy of a corporate culture of *reflexive obedience* and undertake the hard work of creating a culture of *learned willingness* and *individual accountability*.

• Finally, and most difficult, we must embrace the great paradox of the human will: that most often, especially in moments of great danger or opportunity, *the only way to gain control is to give it up*. Johnna Torsone, vice president of personnel at Pitney Bowes, put it candidly, "There is a way of showing that giving up power is actually having it. You do it first yourself."

In subsequent chapters, I'll be flagging these "before and after" ways of thinking as they arise in the actual practice of reengineering management. Here I just want to suggest how we can get from "before" to "after," despite the great difficulties of the trip.

We all know from the recent history of GM and IBM what happens when a company gets stuck in "before." Opportunity goes flickering by, scarcely noticed. Management clings tighter and tighter to the old ways. Command and control *from* the top got them *to* the top, management reasons; so command and control from the top will *keep* them on top. "The system is perfectly adaptable to all contingencies," they say to each other, reassuringly. "If the right commands and controls aren't coming out of those offices, then let's just change the people in the offices. The offices themselves are fine—perfect."

Are all successful companies then doomed to extinction? I had to answer just that question not long ago. I was on a plane with a friend, the then-chairman of one of North America's best-known and most successful financial services companies. He told me what I knew—that his dominance of the marketplace was being forcefully challenged by new and old competitors who were offering dramatically better services at dramatically lower prices. "My managers have never been in this situation before," he said. "All they've ever had to do is increase capacity: add more people, more branch offices, more data centers. Now they've got to make big, painful changes, and I wonder if they're up to it."

My friend was quiet for a moment, then he said, "Tell me, do all good companies have to fail?"

They don't, of course. There's no reason to believe that an implacable fate, or law of entropy, governs human institutions. But many good companies do fail, and many others come hair-raisingly close to failure before they're willing to change. Dave Sanders, a reengineer at Detroit Edison, told us that in talks to his colleagues he always reads off a list of the great companies of the 1950s—Sylvania, for example, or PanAm—that no longer exist, just to remind everyone of how the mighty can fall. Like arrogant navigators, their managers have to feel the surf crashing right over their bows before they change course. Until then, they stick to the methods that gave them mastery.

HOW TO THINK REENGINEERING

So is that it? Companies won't reengineer unless they're about to crash on the rocks?

Well, no. Reengineering is a particular way of using our minds, of *minding* our businesses, and anyone can learn it. It's a way of radical experimentalism, of invention and reinvention, constantly checked by the realities of the bottom line. I sometimes like to think of this mindfulness as peculiarly American, but of course it is not. The men of *virtu* in Renaissance Italy practiced it. The Englishman Francis Bacon wrote eloquently about it in the late 1500s. Adventuresome individuals all over the world, East as well as West, have lived by it. And today, business leaders in Europe and Japan are avid practitioners of it.

Still, I think, no people have had greater or longer experience of the experimental life than Americans have. And no one has expounded it more passionately than America's first and still favorite philosopher, Ralph Waldo Emerson.

Remember his famous line—"A foolish consistency is the hobgoblin of little minds"? It appears in his best read essay, "Self-Reliance," as a reprise of the lesson he was trying to drive home in the previous paragraph. There, he asks us why we are always looking back over our shoulders at what we said or did yesterday. Why do we go on dragging around "this corpse of memory," as Emerson rather brutally describes our conventions, habits, traditions. (Thomas Jefferson, you recall, had some equally harsh things to say about the "dead hand of the past.") We live in a New World, said Emerson, and so we must find a new way of thinking.

"It seems to be a rule of wisdom," he concludes, "never to rely on memory alone . . . but to bring the past for judgment into the thousand-eyed present, and live ever in the light of a new day." I can imagine no more forceful expression of the kind of thinking required in the brave new world of business today. Turn these phrases over in your mind. Savor their astonishing implications:

- A mind perpetually ready to revolt against its own conclusions.
- A mind prepared not for disbelief (nothing so dogmatic) but for a constant, graceful skepticism.
- A mind that's open to any possibility, including impossibility.
- A mind of democratic hospitality to other views (the present has a *thousand* eyes, not just one).
- A mind that is profoundly questioning, but buoyantly hopeful.
- A mind willing and able to bring established processes, procedures and, yes, people to *judgment*.
- A mind easy in the conviction that the verdict on any course of action is brought in, finally, not by Science, not by Reason, not by Technology, not even by public opinion (i.e., market research), but by *results*.
- A mind that can bear the light of a new day.

This is the state of mind that I call living the question. It requires a lot of acceptance. There are no certain answers, no finalities, securities, closures, or predictabilities. The game is never over. As another great New Englander Robert Frost once wrote: "Sometimes the best way out is through." For managers, make that "Always the only way out is through"—and there is no "out." There is only going through it, and through it, and through it. We do this, we live the question, by experiment. "The voyage of the best ship," Emerson said in the same essay, "is a zigzag line of a hundred tacks." Living the question means taking a tack and following it until the wind dies, or the rocks loom too close.

I'm not a sailor, but I happen to like sailing analogies. A sailing ship, as opposed to a motorboat, has to be used with the utmost tact and strength, because there are so many factors—the wind, the tide, the weather—sailors have no control or command over. Sailing metaphors are truer to life, current business life, than machine metaphors. But they, too, can lead to trouble. They assume, for example, that everyone on board knows where they're going and what they're supposed to do to get there, and that the cargo is marketable. These assumptions can't always be made safely, as we shall see.

Sailing metaphors risk making things seem easy that aren't. There's a cruel irony at the heart of the thinking now required of managers. It's all very well for Emerson, Jefferson, and Peter Drucker (not to mention myself) to urge us to abandon the past—that is, consistency, conformity, the dead hand, the corpse of memory, and the rest of it. But that past is us, and the abandoners are us: We are calling on ourselves to abandon ourselves.

Somewhere, I remember seeing a Bugs Bunny–like character, streaking across the screen. Every few seconds, without missing a step, he unzips his skin and drops it behind—the gray one, the blue one, the pink one, zzzzip and they're gone! That character blurs into Wile E. Coyote. I see him zigging and zagging all over the map searching for Roadrunner, only to find himself, in the violence of his venturesomeness, far out over a cliff, levitating in thin air, feet paddling like crazy.

Change! Down with the past! Revolutionize! Think radically! Lead experimentally! Go out on a limb, go over the cliff! This is good advice in real life, if not in cartoons, especially if we consider the alternatives. Linear thinking, grand strategy thinking, formulaic thinking, conventional thinking, credentialed thinking, produce only comforting illusions, bland rigidities, complacent passivity, all the slow-working recipes for disaster. The fact is we don't know what lies ahead. Our times are all "post-" something—post-industrial, post-modern, post–Cold War—and no one knows what they're "pre-" to. Wile E. Coyote is out there, groping with his toes for solid ground. So are we all.

Americans, every one of us immigrants to an unknown New World, are used to this predicament. When the media finally caught on to the fact that American business was going to come out of the last recession better off than its international rivals, everyone suddenly remembered what the American mentality is really good for. Listen to Leslie Wexner:

> The key challenge facing us in the 90s is the same one that faces us every day: To keep taking the risk of change. Sometimes when you're trying to improve, you break something that's already fixed. But unless you change, and take the risk of failure, you limit your opportunities for success. That's why questioning, probing, and reinventing are so important. That is how we redefined the specialty store business several times . . . and how we will continue to reinvent ourselves in the future.

Americans are good at moving on into a changing, contingent, turbulent, adverse, and largely unpredictable universe. That's the universe we're used to, and we're good at meeting the challenge, (re)making, (re)discovering, (re)presenting—in a word, reengineering—everything, including ourselves. Europeans and Japanese are not as welcoming to radical thought; the past is not a corpse for them, but rather the basis for strong cultures and beliefs. Yet managers in those countries are learning the virtues of New World thinking—learning painfully, but fast.

WHAT REENGINEERING THOUGHTS ARE ABOUT

I've suggested the sort of *minding* that reengineering demands of us. Now I want to outline, briefly, what it is, specifically, we should mind about. If managers today must live the questions in order to prevail, then we must know the questions. I've found that there are four of them. They have to be lived simultaneously, but I present them here in the order of priority:

- What is this business for?
- What kind of culture do we want?
- How do we do our work?
- What kind of people do we want to work with?

My first large question addresses *purpose*: What are we aiming at here? What's the point of doing this? Who is this for? What is the market? Who is the customer? Is there any "the" customer? What business are we (really) in? "Should you be doing it at all?" asked Ralph Spurgin of Limited Credit Services. And if yes, should we reinvent it?

What is this business for? There are three good reasons why this question has arisen in the last few years. The first is that dramatic change is in store, actually or potentially, for all industries, all over the world. And the changes are not only dramatic, they are also unending—remorseless. Technology is playing its usual driver role, especially in communications and robotics. Economic politics within and among nations is tearing up old rules of the game. Governments used to give lip-service, at most, to "free markets." Today, as far as electorates will let them, they're actually forcing businesses to be free by privatizing, deregulating, and lifting trade protections on state-favored industries. The result: a technologically empowered, worldwide competitive free-for-all. But this wild new marketplace obliges managers to ask themselves, continuously, whether what they're doing is worth doing, or whether they should be doing something else. It is perfectly possible, for example, that you could be reengineering your work processes *for the wrong business*.

That doleful risk leads me to the second reason we must ask what our businesses are for. Continuous change in the marketplace means continuous change inside the corporation. Whether or not a radical redefinition of the business is necessary, a radical reengineering of work and management processes is almost certainly demanded. And this cannot be done properly unless managers are absolutely clear about their business' purposes. Reengineering, we remember, should be done from the outside in. We first ask, "What business results do we want in the market?"; *then* we ask, "What changes in our core work and management processes must we make to effect those results?"

The third, and last reason, comes from the need and task of leadership. In the Smooth Sailing years, it was believed that only top (and wanna-be top) managers needed to know a corporation's business purposes. No more. Now everyone wants and needs to know what they're in business for. It's not enough for leaders to reply, "We're in business to make money" (who isn't?). And it is *certainly* not enough to say, "We're in business to downsize and outsource, and close plants." If the task of leadership is to rally all members of the organization for continuous revolutionary change, and it is, then leaders must define and express their business purposes in a vivid and compelling way. This means a long, hard living of the question.

What kind of culture do we want? My second large question addresses culture, values, and behavior, asking us managers to develop a set of principles of desired behavior. Here, top managers find themselves in the worst of jams: bearing the final responsibility for a state of affairs over which they have only the most limited control. Their power here is limited not by the precepts of reengineering but by the very nature of a culture. A company's culture cannot be proclaimed or easily manipulated. It consists of the deeply shared values and beliefs of its people, which show up in how the company and its people behave. Look back at our list of "before" and "after" ways of thinking. If these mark the distance between a machine-like culture and a reengineering one, then in many companies we're talking about a veritable voyage to a New World. Managers cannot force this trip on people. At best they can lead the way—that is, they can "model" the behavior, enable it, and educate it, drawing out what is already there, or what they hope is there.

In other words, managers must first change themselves. It is they who have to launch the experimental voyage; they who have to abandon perfectionism and embrace relentless betterment; they who have to have faith in their fellows; they who have to listen to the voice of the people; they who have to learn improvement through "personal best"; they who have to give up the security of tidy charts; they who have to immerse themselves in the culture of learned willingness and individual accountability; they, finally, who have to gain control by giving it up. Managers who cannot get out of the old ways and pass over into the new, will not manage for long.

In Chapter 6, we'll learn how those managers who do make the transition to the New World can help others do likewise.

How do we do our work? Answering that large question was the focus of *Reengineering the Corporation*. But that book dealt with the redesign of our operational processes—again, the processes that have to do with how we invent, manufacture, distribute, sell, and service. Now we must also focus on our managerial processes—the processes through which we manage that value-adding work. When I talk of process in Chapter 8, it will be with an emphasis on these management processes. They are what constitute our day-to-day work, and we must now subject them to the same scrutiny as we have the other work of our companies.

What kind of people do we want to work with? Once again, in the reengineering corporation, there's a new, expanded "we" who must live this question, too. Hiring and promotion, development and deployment, are all now far too important to be left to Human Resources or Personnel alone. For one thing, in the new pluralist corporation, where authority is more and more vested not in "offices" but in skills (often times in teams of variously skilled people), "the kind of people we want to work with" is a question that must be shared, if not monopolized, by the people doing that particular work. Managers unilaterally deploy team-members only at the risk of destroying team morale—that is, at the risk of doing harm to the business.

On the other hand, there are large issues of process and procedure surrounding the "people question" that can only be defined and tentatively resolved by managers of the enterprise. Like everything else in the new corporation, hiring, development, and deployment are no longer one-function processes.

They, too, must be subjected to the same questioning as our operational processes, to see what other *what for's* can be wrung out of them, or tacked onto them. If hiring is just hiring, it could well be (as with contingent workers it is) outsourced. By the same token, if advancing to more complex work were just "promotion," people could be selected by independently administered examinations.

But of course most hiring and development processes are *for*, or can be made to be *for*, much more than that. Above all they can be used as a means of acculturation. In Chapter 10, I'll have occasion to show how many "reengineers" do just that.

These questions of purpose, principles of behavior, process, and people are not new. We managers have been concerned with them for a long time. But I am arguing in this book that today—and for what I expect will be our management lifetime—these questions will define a manager's work.

But what about all those other questions of management that have occupied us for years? What happens to strategy—that endless search for distinctiveness, for the big idea that will bring us riches, for the intelligent understanding of irrational markets? What happens to our fascination with structure, the exercise of moving boxes around on organizational charts as the response to all managerial problems? What do we do with all that investment in systems (mostly information systems) that support our old way of doing business?

There is still validity in examining questions of strategy, structure, and systems. But to a great degree, I see the need, first, to live the questions of purpose, culture, process, and people. It's our purpose and operational capabilities (a.k.a. processes) that will point the way to strategy. It's our purpose and processes that will suggest an optimum (if there is one) structure. And it's our processes and culture that will dictate how we want to design (and continually redesign) our systems. If you haven't gotten it by now, let me say it plainly: Purpose, culture, process, and people replace strategy, structure, and systems as our superordinate questions.

I want to close this chapter with a challenge. Listen to the CEO of a hugely successful food and drink company as he tries to capture his corporation's spirit. "At the end of every day of every year, two things remain unshakable," Roberto C. Goizueta, chairman and CEO of Coca-Cola Co., says. "Our constancy of purpose and our continuous discontent with the immediate present."

Note the contradiction, the inconsistency, the zig and the zag between *constancy* and *discontent*. No hobgoblins, no corpses hold back this company. I've never read a more succinct illustration of what it means to "think reengineering." And neither have I read a more vivid illustration of the *character* required to think reengineering. Somebody once said that the best sign of intelligence is the ability to hold two good, but contradictory ideas in one's head at the same time. More is required of management today than intelligence. Character is required, and the best sign of it—the reengineering character anyway—is not only to hold two good, contradictory ideas, but to act on them. That's the challenge of the remainder of this book.

CHAPTER 4

WHAT IS THIS BUSINESS FOR, ANYWAY?

*Let's go back to what this book is for. It's to help managers
harness the power of the changes that are sweeping the
business world—and sweeping our ranks with it.
How does this book help? By providing managers with the
concepts and tools to reengineer their own management
work, so that they can create business opportunity and
compete successfully for the favors of our customers.
This chapter is devoted to the greatest management tool of
all: leadership.
And to the newest responsibility of leadership: to explain
what's going on. To everyone.*

Reengineering begins with a strategic imperative: Anticipate—
better yet, initiate—the currents and cross currents of customer
demands, needs, and wants. The market may be "customer-

driven" as never before in history; but customers, being only
human, often do not know what they demand, need, want,
unless and until they see it. This gives companies a good deal of
opportunity to shape their markets—once their managers understand what's going on.

And this market flow is *out there*. The reengineering of management asks managers at all levels to get out of their command-
posts, out of the boxes on the organization chart, out to where
the real world of business lies—in the marketplace. But with that
outward movement, everything in the enterprise must change.

Why? Because markets and customers are always changing.
Relentlessly, customers ratchet up their demands on every front:
price, quality, service, novelty, timeliness. At the same time, we
must also respond to and take advantage of changes in our
industries, changes driven both by technology and by political
and social reform. But to do all this requires the mobilization of
the entire enterprise, and it is this mobilization that begins radical change within the organization.

We know what these changes entail: All operations must be
submitted to a thorough critique of their usefulness—of their very
existence—in terms of the value they produce for the company—
value that must eventually be judged in markets by customers.
All employees (including those in all remaining levels of management) must put themselves through a continuous questioning of
how their work adds value. And finally (perhaps firstly), if all
these radical changes are to come about, there may have to be
an equally radical change in the culture of the enterprise.

In this chapter, we're going to look at what it takes to help a
corporation mobilize for the total struggle that today's chaotic
markets and customer-driven competition demands. It takes leadership, of course, but leadership of a new kind. I mean the capacity to articulate the reasons—the *motivating explanations*—why
this business and its people must do what they're being called on
to do. Several levels of reasons are due, as we shall see, but they
all respond to questions on the minds of all employees everywhere these days. These questions revolve around a business's
purpose: "What is this business for?" "What's in it for me, for
the industry, for the customer?" "What are we all doing here,
anyway?"

People work for a paycheck, sure. But if that's the only reason they can find for going to work every day, they won't work with the imagination, the resourcefulness, the steady willingness, and the sensitivity to the marketplace that we've got to promote all the way through the organization if we want to prevail in today's environment.

In this book I'll use the word "purpose," rather than "mission," because it suggests a more fundamental examination of the business. But the job for management is two-fold: First, our times require us to reexamine and restate our business purpose; and second, we must use this restatement to fully mobilize our companies for change. In prior times, we referred to these jobs as the "hard" work of strategy, and the "soft" work of changing behavior. But as you will see from the testimony of two relatively "hard-headed" managers, it no longer serves us to think of some things as "hard" and others as "soft." Such differentiation will diminish one or the other, depending on your view of what's important. To bring about change today, managers must do both; the "hard" and the "soft" are equally important.

Who's going to answer the questions every business must ask itself? The response used to be obvious—the CEO, the enterprise manager, the leader. It's still obvious, at least with respect to one key question: Only the enterprise manager has the authority to decide what business the company is in. His authority in this matter is derived from the fact that investors, shareholders, their representatives (a.k.a. the board of directors), and the public will eventually hold the CEO accountable for it. If that were the end of the matter, we'd still be in the era of Smooth Sailing. But we're not. The fact is that with authority now being redistributed throughout the organization, there is no *the* leader. Everyone must be a leader; everyone, that is to say, must answer questions about the business's purpose—and ask questions, too. As the CEO of one company told me, "Everyone here must be able to give the 'elevator talk.' That is, explain what business we're in during the time it takes to get from one floor to the next."

But there's another key question that only the CEO can answer. This is the question of *when*—when to begin the process of reengineering, the process that goes on to continuous mobilization, continuous change, and continuous questioning and answering *why?*, *what for?* So let me begin with *when*, too.

LIVING THE QUESTION OF WHEN TO REENGINEER

There's always a precipitating event, or occasion, which leadership can seize upon to begin the task of reengineering. And unfortunately it's almost always the same event—an impending business disaster. The only difference, from company to company, is how near to disaster the business has come. (There are, of course, a few companies in which leadership has been so strong that disaster is kept at a considerable distance. Usually, though, these are companies that are already in a constant state of mobilized alertness to the threats and opportunities of their marketplace.)

Fifty-year-old Richard Abdoo of the Wisconsin Energy Corp., the largest utility in the state, thought that his company was a long way from ruin. When Abdoo became CEO in 1989, according to his own account, his board of directors proudly announced that they were bestowing on him what they considered "an absolutely great company."

They were not wrong. The utility had revenues of nearly $2 billion, assets of about $4 billion, a market capitalization of almost $3 billion, and a double-A bond rating which they'd had "almost forever." (Before that, it was triple-A, which bond raters don't give anymore.) Earnings were "good"; dividend payout "exceeded the average." The regulators were pleased by their rates, which had been reduced every time the utility had gone before the Public Service Commission. The environmental people were happy. In short, "everybody thought we were doing great," Abdoo remembers.

But Abdoo knew better. After making a mental tour of his real bosses in the free market, and of his rivals for their favors, Abdoo was reminded of a bit of wisdom he'd learned long ago— that complacency led to mediocrity, which led to failure. That made him worry as he looked to the future. "Uh oh; you've got a big problem," he told himself. "If you follow that path, you're still going to be here at age 60, and you're going to be at a point in your life when you will want to continue to be here. Then they're going to tell you that they don't want you anymore, because you took this perfectly good company that was on top of the world, and wrecked it."

Fortune once laid down a rule about reengineering: that there are only two reasons anyone ever undertakes it, greed and fear. And the greatest of these, the new CEO might have added, is fear.

As far as Abdoo could see, at Wisconsin Energy, he was the only one who was afraid—and that was the scariest challenge of all. Most of the employees "believed that what they were doing was absolutely the right thing to do," he recalls. So how on earth was he going to persuade them otherwise, convince them that they'd have to change virtually everything they did and thought and were?

Lots of enterprise managers have faced the same problem. From Abdoo's perspective, the business needed what Lawrence Bossidy, chairman and CEO of AlliedSignal, calls "a burning platform"—except that, not having found one already afire, Abdoo would have to light it. Or he would have to "drop a bomb," as William Weiss, former chairman and CEO of Ameritech, calls it. Or, if I may put the thing in tea-party language, he would have to "share his misgivings" with his colleagues. But whatever we call it, the effective meaning is the same: He would have to start mobilizing his company.

He started, mistakenly as it turned out, at the top. He gave his top 100 managers at the 5,650-employee company, including all the officers, a Christmas present, a book by Judy Barwick called *Danger in the Comfort Zone*. It did indeed arouse a good deal of apprehension among Abdoo's direct reports, but none of them saw the dangers clearly, or were willing to risk their own comfort to address them. "Those managers were the easiest to deal with," he remembers. "They pursued career opportunities elsewhere in short order." Inevitably, some prefer to move on rather than change.

The next echelon down proved almost as disappointing. These managers "got it" all right, but didn't seem to grasp the fact that it was up to them to do something about it. At that point, Abdoo realized that if he wanted any help in his mobilization effort, he'd never find it by observing the usual hierarchical chain of command. So he skipped over two levels of management to find eight "best and brightest kids." These were people, he liked to josh, who'd been "picking lettuce" only weeks before. Together they set out to redesign the whole company.

Flash forward 15 months. As of the summer of 1994 he and the "kids" had accomplished two of the three stages in their reengineering effort. They had sketched out, in broad conceptual strokes, the kind of company they wanted to work in, given the nature of their market. They'd also called in a reengineering consultant to draw up the blueprint for the new structure. Now they were facing stage three—the actual construction process.

It sounds straightforward, but Abdoo remembers it as the challenge of his career:

> There is only one word to describe the transition—*hell*. From doing things very, very successfully, being a leader, on top, we had to go down into the pit, if you will, in order to come out the other side; moving faster, better, with higher targets, is a hell to go through. . . . There are times when I find this job more fulfilling than I ever anticipated, and there are other times when I wonder, "What am I doing here? Do I really need to go through this hell?" But those bad days don't occur very often. Most of it is upbeat and very, very positive.

Dick Abdoo told his story at a utilities conference in St. Louis in July of last year. Also at the conference was the CEO of another utility, Mark DeMichele of Arizona Public Service. DeMichele's story ended very much like his colleague's—but the beginning couldn't have been more different.

APS was headed straight for disaster. What's more, everyone knew it. As the builder of the largest nuclear power plant in the "free world," as one employee put it, the company had had a public relations problem for years. Then in the late 1980s, the company's CEO set up a holding company in order to diversify. This was not unusual. Wisconsin Energy is similarly "held." But

APS chose to diversify by buying a savings and loan bank—just in time for the devastating real estate crash of 1988. As real estate values plummeted, and the S&L went into receivership, the price of APS stock took a nose-dive, along with the life-savings (in homes and shares) of many of the company's 9,000 employees. Layoffs began, outraging the community and the media. Prices went up, outraging the regulators. Seeing its opportunity, PacifiCorp. of Portland, Oregon, began a hostile take-over bid.

This sort of thing was not supposed to happen to a utility. Power companies, gas companies, phone companies—these monopolies, or near monopolies, are America's equivalent of Europe's and Japan's state-supported industries—U.S. Volvo companies, if you like, or Air France. Even more than GM or IBM, utilities are perfect representations of the "machine"-like corporation that flourished between 1917 and 1973. They were designed to "go of themselves," guaranteeing lifetime jobs for employees and a perpetual profit. Ameritech's former CEO William Weiss recalled what it was like in the Bell System before Judge Green broke it up: "People believed that if you got a job here, it was a lifetime opportunity. We had an entitlement philosophy, believing that we were a monopoly, because it was right to be a monopoly. Many people thought competitive entry was a bad thing. Their inclination was to hang onto the things that had kept us so secure in the past."

That was the inclination of people at APS, too. Mark DeMichele recalled that by the end of the decade, APS qualified not only as a disastrous corporation but as an insane one, too—insane in that it did the same thing over and over, expecting one set of results and always getting another. In other words, it was the same at APS, under disastrous circumstances, as it was at the Wisconsin utility, under auspicious circumstances: Nobody wanted to change, or could change.

The only thing that would do the trick, DeMichele was convinced, was leadership. What he means by that much-abused concept owes nothing to the command-and-control ideology of the corporate "machine." Instead it depends on his behavior, his ability to build bridges of trust linking APS into a "we." From the outset of his mobilization effort, DeMichele understood that the most important (and least discussed) asset of any leader is followers, and that followers are not to be commanded and controlled but understood. To mobilize a company, the leader must learn the needs of its people, articulate them, and, in the deepest sense of the word, *respond* to them. Only thus can leaders meet what DeMichele calls the "pre-reengineering challenge."

"If your organization isn't change-ready, reengineering is going to be very, very painful, and just simply won't be anywhere near as effective as it could be, or should be," he told the St. Louis gathering. "That's where every one of us as leaders needs to focus our energies."

WHO WANTS TO KNOW?

Whatever precipitates the mobilization for change, the first duty of leadership is to understand people's need-to-know, to understand where they fit into the immediate and long-term purposes of the business. This may sound either patronizing or prostrating, but it's neither, simply a matter of good business judgment—in fact, of self-preservation. The would-be mobilizer for change who fails to figure out the employees' deepest needs at this critical juncture in their work-lives, or who fails in the most literal way *to speak to* those needs, will only intensify and extend the struggle for change.

To whom must the CEO *speak*? Let me be clear about this, even at the risk of being repetitive: everybody in and around the corporation—managers, non-managers (a vanishing breed anyway), vendors, the surrounding community(s), investors, and, needless to say, the customers.

This may seem excessive; some managers may not see it as a natural act. After all, in the old days of command-and-control, it was part of the adversarial set-up between "management" and "labor" that managers *knew* and labor *did* (after contract negotiations) what it was told to do. Managers had a huge stake at issue in this arrangement. Our progress up the hierarchy was measured not only in salary differentials, perks, privileges, and the number of our direct reports, it was also measured in what we knew about what the company was doing and was about to do—the "big picture." This (elevated) knowledge was the sign and substance of our (elevated) standing in the organization. And while it was assumed that some people, mostly lower level managers, would envy us our knowledge, it was also assumed that everyone else, "labor," "workers," etc., didn't care.

To some extent these assumptions were accurate. The adversarial culture had labor especially role-bound. When the seas started to get rough in the 1970s and 1980s, managers tried sharing something of what they knew. But their increasingly plaintive cries—"we're all in the same boat," "time to batten down the hatches, get ship-shape"—fell on deaf ears. Labor was frozen in its adversarial posture by its investments in the seniority system, the grievance system, the work-rule system (union Taylorism). Nor could it forget management's own long devotion to the adversarial culture.

There were other problems with these cries. To the worker, they were (and still are) abstractions. Because management either didn't really understand what was going on, or if they did chose not to share it, workers could only hear the distress calls as vacuous cliches.

Mobilization for today must be total mobilization, up, down, and sideways. This means that everyone must be "in the know." Unless they are, you can forget about getting a total mobilization; in fact, everyone *not* in-the-know will see nothing in your efforts but a conspiracy. No one is going to go through the ordeal of a total mobilization for change without knowing why, or what for. The successful manager today isn't the one who is entrusted with secrets, but the manager who wins trust by sharing what he or she knows.

It's only when people trust us that we can mobilize them for the brutal changes required by reengineering. (For that matter, it's only when we're trusted that we win the hearts, minds, and wallets of our customer.) But to gain that trust, we must be candid, forthright, open—with everybody. If that seems like lowering our defenses and throwing away some hard-won status, that's the point. Knowledge is power. Help, if it is to be effective, requires power. Managers need effective help. Therefore, managers have to share all the knowledge we have. Michael Walsh, the late chairman and CEO of Tenneco, said it straight: "To win trust, you've got to make yourself vulnerable."

WHAT DO THEY WANT TO KNOW?

On the threshold of radical change, what people really want to know is just what we all want to know—that our fears are unjustified, that we're going to be safe forever.

Time was, in the days of Smooth Sailing, when many managers could actually come close to giving such assurances. I know a master machinist whose father and grandfather each worked for more than 50 years in the same company where he worked for 23 years. But in today's competitive climate, to promise that kind of security is unrealistic. And as we've seen, if there's anything that we reengineering practitioners agree on, it is that no one, in any company, in any market, is ever going to be completely safe again.

This is not a soothing state of affairs for those who worry about the stability of our societies. But today the manager's immediate worry must lie elsewhere—in arousing people to get set for a radically different state of affairs in the corporation. That manager may not be able to provide soothing words, but he or she can provide the next best thing—reasons and a picture of the future. Everyone wants reasons and that picture, and in the reengineering effort everyone had better have them.

Big Picture Reasons

A surprising number of the reengineering managers we talked to recalled that whatever procedures they eventually used to prepare the company for change—usually some sort of "focus" group, like the DELTA ("Develop Excellence through Leadership, Teamwork, and Accountability") classes that Dick Abdoo set up—they never failed to cite history. Abdoo says he worked up his own resolve by looking back, "I saw the General Motors, and the IBMs, and the Westinghouses of the world, who dominated their industry a decade or so ago, and saw the difficulty they were in . . ."

The history lesson produces a good scare—that past success does not guarantee future success—but there's nothing wrong with that. For one thing, capitalism is a system that quite literally *works* on fear. For another thing, the only way to persuade many folks to undertake a painful therapy like reengineering, followed by a permanent state of mobilization, is to persuade them that the alternative will be even more painful. With IBM and GM still around, we have living examples of the alternative—and of the fact that it's not always ruin.

Some managers no doubt use this reasoning from the historical context as a way of saying, "Look, I know reengineering is hard, but it's not our fault; history is making us do it." This is a ploy that should be used with great caution, though the premise is not entirely false. History *is* at work here: nudging, prodding, threatening. But history doesn't tell us how to respond, that we must decide on our own. People know this, and will hold you accountable for whatever choices you make.

The Big Picture argument is not supposed to settle anything—least of all the question of "why we had to do it," when the "it" in question is reengineering. It simply begins the mobilization process in a way that establishes the same horizon for everyone, the actual world-historical horizon of business today. This is a good thing to do, not only as a reason behind the reengineering process, but also as a way of providing everyone with a larger meaning for the enterprise, and for themselves within the enterprise. We may not all be in the same boat: industries, corporations, people differ, and in non-superficial ways. But we are all laboring in the same ocean.

Industry-Specific Reasons

Well, maybe *not* in the same ocean. Some of us are in the North Atlantic, some in the South Pacific, and so on. We are, after all, in different industries, and although almost every industry is going through some change, not all changes are of the same kind in every industry. For reengineering and mobilization purposes, it is vital to be clear about what changes are demanded by what causes in your specific industry.

Industries today are being compelled to change by either technological or socio-political developments, or by some combination of the two. If you're in the media industry (print, radio, cable, television), clearly it's information and communications technology that's driving the change. If you're in health care, it's a political demand for reform *and* technology that are doing it. If you're with a utility company, it's "politics" again: Deregulation is adding a novel competition to your industry. It's the same if you're in a government-owned airline (e.g., Air France): Privatization is about to change your life.

This makes it sound simpler than it will be for many managers, especially those of us who have been so focused on the "internalities" of our companies that we don't really understand what's going on in our industries' markets. We've been lulled into thinking that we could run our corporate machines without really understanding their business. That's especially true the more you moved up in the old hierarchy of the company.

Recently I was called by an executive search firm that had been engaged by a large computer software company to recruit a new CEO. The current CEO, the founder, was considered not to have the management skills needed to move the company through its next growth phase. The recruiter asked whether I knew anyone who might fill the "slot." I asked how much knowledge of the market was required. "Little" was the answer; they were looking for a manager who had run a large company. Well, fortunately, I didn't hold stock in that software company. If I had, I would have sold it fast.

The good news is that you can gain experience by getting out and walking around the market. One company I know requires every one of its managers (including the CEO) to answer the customer 800 service phone for two hours a month. Other managers do it without prompting. But whatever your technique, understanding and explaining what's going on in your industry is today a critical job of managers, all managers.

Corporation-Specific Reasons

For some managers, the sense of a common world, bounded by a common horizon, is so powerful that it leads them to believe that everybody's response to it will be equally common. Common world, common sense: What else is there to say? I think, for example, of the CEO of an extremely successful computer software company who had some scornful things to say about reengineering. "It's all bull," he once remarked. "Come on, it all comes down to management keeping in touch with customers. There are no models. Use your common sense."

This is fine, so long as the gentleman understands that his common sense and mine, which I drew on to come up with the (to me) commonsensical notions of reengineering, may differ. I'm sure that he and his associates share a set of precepts, customs, symbols, and, yes, "models" of doing business. If so, these things add up to *their* common sense; that is, to *their* culture (a deeply cultivated common sense). But their common sense, their culture, cannot be assumed to be common to, say, their major competitor. Such an assumption belongs to the past, to the days of the corporate "machine" and the professional know-how of the accredited MBA. I worry when I hear managers say "it's just common sense" or "it's time to get back to basics." These broad, seemingly hard-headed statements deny the complexity of today's markets, the changes our industries are going through, and the new demands of customers. Today, the only "basics" we may have to operate with may be trust, integrity, imagination, and a cooperative spirit.

I wouldn't deny that at a certain level of abstraction many managers, even across many different industries, can understand each other perfectly well. Nevertheless, the fact remains that when the era of Smooth Sailing came to an end, and the Rough Seas started rising, the waves scattered the old beliefs we called "common sense" all over the map, just as they did all other forms of security. Nowadays what we have in common is not a "sense" but a marketplace of "senses," all bidding for the attention of specific managers in conducting specific organizations in specific markets.

It's this irreducible specificity that must also be sounded, along with the "big picture," by any manager who wants to mobilize a company for change. If the enterprise is in trouble, people want to know in just what ways it's in trouble—all the whos, whys, hows, and how muches.

It may seem to top management that everyone already knows these things. After all, as the media gets smarter about business news, most of us are now sailing along in ships-in-a-bottle with every tack and jibe in plain sight. But the truth is that what people "know," especially in times of trouble, gets increasingly distorted by fears, fantasies, and first-person reasoning. Managers must address these concerns. And little, if anything, should be held back when they do so. The details of the trouble, the facts and figures—these have a central place in the mobilization process. In his St. Louis talk, Mark DeMichele described the work he did at Arizona Public Service:

> In five-day sessions with managers, and three-day sessions with frontline people, we confronted the pain of what we'd been through [the take-over struggle, etc.], and the problems of our current culture.

Purpose and Vision

DeMichele's next sentence marks a pivotal moment—the Emersonian moment, if you will—in the mobilization effort. "Plus," he said, "we started questioning who we wanted to become." Here is the radical turning point of the reengineering mind, when we leaders must *let go* the impelling past and the perilous present—the "corpse of memory," in Emerson's phrase—and *let in* the "light of a new day."

DeMichele and his reengineering team went so far as to dramatize this pivotal moment at APS with a sort of symbolic burial and rebirth. In the course of putting the past "up for judgment," he not only examined jobs, but the people doing them. "Everybody had to reapply for their job," he said. "They had to be rehired based on the fact that they were the best person for the job. . . . That was kind of scary, because even my job was on the line."

This procedure may seem too theatrical, but it rests on an unavoidable fact, which is that "reengineering does indeed create a significant sense of loss," as DeMichele put it. "Changing the way work gets done [managerial work, too, he might have said] means giving up something that [people have been] comfortable with for a long time." That kind of loss has to be taken seriously. Its passage to the past must be observed in an almost ritual sense. Otherwise, we won't see it "pass," and it won't remain "past."

At the same time, something positive has to be put in place of these losses—if not new securities, then new challenges, new purposes, new passages—*forward*. As I've said, the usual managerial terms for the substance of this pivot to the future are words like "purpose," "mission," or "vision." "What they need," said DeMichele, "is a new vision of their future . . . hope, hope for the future. Letting them know what was expected of them at the new APS, and letting them know where we were headed, and the role that they played in our new strategic plan."

The need for this sort of thing is sometimes denied. In March of 1994, for example, the *New York Times* ran a story about IBM which began with a recollection of a sensational statement that Lou Gerstner made when he came on board in the summer of 1993. "The last thing IBM needs right now," he said, "is a vision." Shock, horror, and consternation greeted this statement in many quarters. I expect that what Gerstner meant was that IBM needed immediate action to correct its business performance—not a long "walk in the woods" to examine its purpose or vision. But his statement can be justified on other grounds. For two generations, IBM had thrived under the singular vision of the two Thomas Watsons, Senior and Junior. The younger man ran the company he'd inherited with the single-minded determination of an old-style shipmaster (his children, who had literally sailed with him, sometimes called him Captain Ahab). His successors followed that vision to the end—on the rocks.

Thus, if that's what "vision" meant at IBM, then Gerstner was right: It was the last thing the company needed. And as we've seen, this is often the case. Emersonian managers know that visions quickly become a hindrance when circumstances change, whereupon it's better to get rid of them.

At the same time, it's still as true as it ever was that "without a vision the people perish." And this is especially true in periods of wrenchingly painful change.

"Values" come in here, too. "We have to provide something for people to hang on to, that doesn't change during the reengineering process," said DeMichele. But values are part of a company's culture, its common sense, and therefore properly belong in the next chapter where we discuss the job of securing the benefits of reengineering by "managing" the culture.

With "purpose" and "vision," the trick is for managerial leaders to hold them lightly, easily, disposably, experimentally, yet also persuasively, powerfully. Nothing else, for mobilization, will do. Managers must thus come up with a compelling image of the company as they want it to be (the vision they have in mind for it) at some time, but not for all time, in the future. The time may be, and often is, specified as a deadline, and the image concentrated in a slogan. As Shirley Richard, a key APS reengineer, told us in an interview: "We began by establishing a vision. Most companies have one but too often it lacks rigor and detail. Our vision in 1991 aimed at a five-year development in five categories—customer service, power plant operations, environment, and the like—and we developed specific requirements in each of them." Richard's lesson is that without measurable milestones—ports of call, if you like—reengineering won't help you. Besides, at APS, the rigor and the detail yielded a nice slogan: "Top Five in '95!"

There's a reassuring ring to *numbers*. APS's leadership put the company on the line with those words. They chose five commensurable benchmarks of excellence, and asked to be judged by the progress they'd made toward being among the top five contenders in their industry. This takes guts, but it also provides employees with a kind of intellectual security that managers should make the most of.

With numbers we can also know where we stand in relation to everyone else along common measures of performance. Numbers are the substance of what I think of as the navigational rhetoric of managerial leadership—the rhetoric of accountancy, basically, as opposed to the inspirational rhetoric of ordinary language. Both are required. But one other reason that "vision" is a word in some disfavor today is that it conjures up soft pictures of the future. Numbers—metrics, if you will—make statements of vision more substantive.

Purpose and Vision II

Navigational rhetoric, however necessary, is never sufficient. People are reassured by numbers, scores, bottom lines. But numbers by themselves never mobilized anyone but an accountant, or not for long. For that we need purposes and visions made out of a more inspirational rhetoric of concepts and metaphors.

Some of these words, in the form of metaphors, can transform not only the image (and self-image) of a company, but also its practices. We've seen this truth amply illustrated, in negative fashion, by the vision of a corporation as a machine. Now let's look at some positive versions of the same story. The reader may want to turn to the following chapter for examples of a whole variety of transforming images with which corporate leaders have galvanized their companies for change and a fresh shot of competitive energy. Here I'll focus on two especially dramatic metaphorical metamorphoses.

First, consider what happened to PepsiCo's Pizza Hut division in the mid-1980s, when 90 percent of the growth in the pizza-chain business was being gobbled up by Domino's. Until then, Pizza Hut's managers had thought they were a chain of restaurants. But Domino's challenge persuaded them that they'd better change the metaphor from one that conjured up a picture of people sitting in a restaurant enjoying a meal to one that implied the food being served in a variety of locations: malls, airports, museums, etc. In short, the "restaurant" chain became a "distribution system."

Never underestimate the power of a good metaphor. Soon, Pizza Hut began to license restaurant service operations in partnership with companies like Host Marriott, the better to concentrate on its core business of preparing and carrying foods faster and farther afield. Revenues more than doubled. The next step seems clear, at least by metaphorical logic. Once you've built a food transportation system, why stop at exalted pizzas?

Pizza Hut may now move other foods—sometimes directly to customers and sometimes through its partnerships. After that, who knows what foods may go through their distribution channels?

Our second metaphorical metamorphosis occurred when Leonard Riggio started to think of his Barnes & Noble chain of bookstores as a chain of "theaters." After years in the discount and remaindered book business, Riggio suddenly had a vision of the actual reasons people frequent bookstores. It is the same reason why people go to the theater (as opposed to sitting in the dark at the movies, or sitting at home watching TV). They go because going to the theater is basically a *social* experience. It's the same at bookstores: People like going to bookstores (as opposed to ordering books from a catalogue, in some ways a less bothersome task) because they like being among people who like books.

Once the metaphor took hold, it wouldn't let up. Everything at Barnes & Noble had to change to accommodate it. The salespeople had to become personable and solicitous, as opposed to "snotty" (the salespeople of bookstores in Riggio's youth) or invisible (the salespeople in the "old" Barnes & Noble). The decor had to change, too: It had to be impressive, spacious, chock full of every kind of book—in a word, dramatic. Most important, if going to Barnes & Noble was to be a social experience, he had to make room for people to be with each other in reasonable comfort. Thus, all over the superstores are nooks and crannies, with chairs and tables, where people can browse and scope out the crowd, or even snooze. There are also cafes for, as it were, intermission time. The *New York Times*'s recent story on the B&N on 82nd Street and Broadway noted that the place had become one of the most appealing and active singles scenes in the city.

Pizza Hut and Barnes & Noble, however, perfectly illustrate the requirement that inspirational visions of a company must be left open to revision, and revision, and revision. What happens to a bookstore "theater" if socializing should become the only thing that goes on there? (A friend tells me that the Broadway B&N actually looks less like a theater than a college library at exam time; that is, not a commercial venue at all.) By the same token, what happens to a food transportation system when the customers start complaining about the service of the contract feeders?

But the perishability of specific metaphors, of concrete purposes by no means lets manager-leaders off the hook. As DeMichele told us:

> There's a fine line between heaven (that's the opportunities reengineering brings) and hell (that's the stress and strain and fear of change). Leaders have to be able to tip that emotional scale, both psychologically and in a real sense, in favor of the positive. Constant restructuring is, I think, going to be a way of life in this business from this day forward, and the challenge for leadership during reengineering is to acknowledge the stress, to support [the people who remain], and to keep them focused on the positive, keep them focused on the future.

Personal Meaning

Ultimately, what the manager aims at doing with his or her expression of the purpose of the company, whether it's expressed in substantive numbers or inspirational rhetoric or catchy metaphors, is to mobilize the talent and energies of people—first in the company and then extending outward to suppliers and vendors. This can't be done without first establishing what the business is for, where it fits in a commercial scheme of things, and where its managers hope it will fit. But beyond this, the manager's vision aims to arouse each and every employee to the task. And this can be done only by establishing a sense of personal significance—significance in and to the corporation—in the hearts and minds of every employee. This significance lies partly in how the new purpose and vision will affect our work and partly in changing the culture of a reengineering company. The latter is the subject of Chapter 6. But I'll close this chapter with a simple observation. A manager's statement of purpose and vision is important in this task of *signification*. It's the master script, if you will, in which we all play out our different roles. It's the corporate meaning in which we find our personal meaning.

CHAPTER 5

CASES IN POINT—HOW WE DECIDED

*Making an operation change-ready, like all of the
reengineering that will follow, starts with a question—what,
and who, is this business really for?
But asking the question is only a necessary first step.
Answers must be found, out in the real world, with
customers, suppliers, partners, investors, and employees.
Then those answers must be shared, spread by managers
who take up the mobilizing mission as their own.*

Developing purpose and vision used to be considered the job of
the CEO alone, the one true leader. And even today, it is with
the enterprise manager that the mobilization for change must
begin. But in tumultuous times like ours, asking the leadership
questions with which that process begins must be the work of all
managers.

The questions are hard, and answering them is often painful,
but everyone must understand the urgency which they demand:

- What do you see in your markets? How will changes in technology and political and social reform transform your industry? What does it mean to operate globally (really)? To have global competition? What input does this provide for developing the case for change in your own company?

- What is the historical context in which you are operating? What can you learn from the past? How can you teach from the past?

- What capabilities will be specifically needed to operate in the future, in your industry, as it will be redefined? How will these operating capabilities make you distinctive?

- What is your business for, who is it trying to serve, and how should it go about serving them? Can you develop a contemporary statement of purpose and vision, made substantive by the metrics which describe your objectives? Can you create a metaphor for change, an image of the future that can spread throughout the organization, inspiring everyone for the hard work to come?

Let me show how asking those questions—and trying to answer them—has worked.

Usually it is the enterprise manager who will see the need for change first, and most dramatically, and who must begin the process of mobilizing the entire company. That process begins with a clear-eyed look to the future, as well as to the present and past—and often starts with fear.

Lawrence English, president, CIGNA HealthCare: When I became president, we were already in the midst of very substantial market change. We were faced with many competitors, all of whom were clamoring for our marketshare.

Historically, CIGNA has been one of the nation's premier writers of group insurance, with a long heritage of business-to-business relationships, very focused on our indemnity instruments and our fiduciary responsibilities to large companies. To the extent we dealt with individual consumers, we dealt indirectly through the benefits managers and decision-makers of these companies.

Our focus was mainly inward: We asked questions that only had relevance to us, not our customers. In fact, it often seemed we studiously avoided asking how well we were meeting the needs of customers. We had a culture that was attuned to the old indemnity world, where the corporate customer was king.

That's no longer the case. In our new business—directly providing managed health care to millions of individuals—both the employer and each individual employee are critically important to us, both now have the ability to exercise his or her own personal choice. And with the right kind of reform—reform in which the marketplace is allowed to work unfettered—individuals will have more choices and more competition.

We would have to transform what had been an indemnity, administrative, and financing company for business into what will be a health care delivery system for people. So we would have to look at our processes and products in terms of how well they satisfy the customer, how they affect the customer's perception of quality. Our whole orientation would have to shift to the consumer, because our business now shares in the individual life and death decisions of people's lives.

Although we had two million members in our HMOs, no one internally had firmly and clearly articulated the vision that at some point in the future we will no longer be an organization that pays claims and finances and administers group insurance plans; we will be an integrated health care delivery system. The company had done a reasonably good job of recognizing that change was taking place, but employers in this country who were paying the bills for health care felt like they were paying too much and impairing their competitiveness, while their employees were unhappy about the service and paperwork.

We had a management team who had been very successful in the indemnity world for a long time, with the structure of an indemnity insurance company: a sales department, claims department, administration department, underwriting department. There was no integration of the business; in some markets the head of sales had never met the head of the health plan operation. But if you want to become an integrated health care delivery system, they are essential to one another's success.

But structure wasn't the only issue. We needed an attitude adjustment, too. In the indemnity world, we could often charge our expenses back to our customers, so we lacked expense discipline. Again, it was very clear to me that our cost-plus attitude had to go, along with an infrastructure that wasn't suited to our new vision.

So we were determined to create a company that is characterized by three things: first, the superiority of the product we deliver to customers, as measured by customers. The measurement will not be how fast you process the mail, but how the claimant felt about the transacton. Second, high-performance, high-energy, hardworking people in this organization; I wanted people who will roll up their sleeves and get out in the field and get the work done, not a bunch of bureaucrats enriching themselves and delegating the hard work to consultants. Third, outstanding financial returns for the shareholder, which comes from taking care of the customer. We needed to recognize that profitability is the real measure of adding value. That was very important to us.

I'm convinced that we will profit if we do these things well. If we do it right, the rewards are going to be enormous—and I'm not speaking of personal financial rewards, but the rewards for all of us in being part of something that is critically important to our society.

It is not enough for a leader to have a vision. A leader needs to attract followers (or, as I prefer to call them, "associates"), men and women who can commit themselves to the new ideal (and necessity) of customer focus. But if the mobilization process is to succeed, those followers must become leaders, too, finding their own sense of purpose in the shared challenge, and spreading the call and vision of change.

Lawrence English: I said to my staff, we are going to become a health care delivery system. The actual form will evolve over time, but our three central characteristics of superior product, people, and profit are non-negotiable. If you don't like them, then find someplace else to work.

To get our vision, we've necessarily had to make a number of changes in senior management. I was looking for people who understood the new vision, who were committed to it and were prepared to do the things that needed doing so that we could achieve it.

It's never easy making personnel decisions, and in this instance it was even more difficult. I'd grown up in the company with some of these people for over 30 years; I had a lot of friends among them. But we had to make changes to break up the institutional consciousness—the mind block—that exists in an organization as old and as big as ours. And I think that, among much of the rank and file, the reaction to the changes was positive. It served as a sign that the days of an isolated, arrogant, old-boy management were over.

The people I brought in were change advocates. I brought in Faerie Kizzire, a woman who'd had a significant hand in creating Sprint's customer service operation. I put her in charge of our claims department and our administration department, which we were planning to merge.

I said we aren't just a claim payer anymore; we have customers out there who want to call in and get immediate answers about their treatment or how to change doctors. We have to have people who are trained to answer those questions and trained in the telephone skills needed to make the caller happy. Without those people, we'd never achieve our business goals.

Faerie Kizzire, senior vice president, National Service Organization, CIGNA HealthCare: When I first came here, I asked to see a flow chart of the customer life cycle, showing who was primarily responsible at each step in the cycle. It took about eight weeks to get it back: down the left side of the page were the elements of both the national service organization and the company's operating units. As you read across, you went through the customer's life cycle. At almost every point of customer contact, every functional part of the organization was involved. Each part of the company had set up its own check points for every significant customer-related event. For every decision made, every component had to sign off. Everyone was accountable, and so no one was accountable.

In the past people here put a lot of value on complexity—they were actually proud that the work was so hard and complex that no one could do it. My reaction was, who are we kidding? If we can't do it, the customer won't be satisfied, and so what is the purpose? Why aren't we trying to make it as simple as we can?

To change this situation, we've identified the critical business processes that affect the customer's perception of quality. For a particular process, such as determining eligibility, we have identified a number of inputs, a number of steps, and a definite output. And we have an owner—whom we call the 'process champion'—who controls all the steps, who is accountable for the final output, and who does not have to review every decision with each department head along the way. The process champion works for the customer, not the organizational heads.

We're not just changing our business, we're changing how we do business. It starts with a clean piece of paper and asking ourselves how can we simplify things, how can we go to an all-electronic claims service, how can we automate other services, how can we do things simpler, faster, more productively.

Previously my organization consisted of two divisions, administration and claims, which had very little understanding of each other. Nor was there any accountability for process results. Now we've reshaped them into a single organization that deals respectively with employer and employee services.

When I arrived here, we started by spending a lot of time defining a vision of where we were headed, building a team. First we elaborated the critical concepts:

1. We value all our customers, both external and internal;

2. We must be intolerant of mediocrity;

3. Teamwork is essential to our success, especially as we reengineer from a hierarchical structure to a self-directed work team structure;

4. We act with integrity in all we do; we are honest and straight with each other, we give fair and frequent feedback;

5. We are determined to win and celebrate our victory—by finding someone doing something right and thanking them, and letting others hear you say that.

Then we defined our vision, which can be stated as follows:

We resolve to set a new standard of excellence as the service leader in our industry.
We will deliver exceptional health care–related services and information, guaranteed to exceed our customers' expectations.
We will do the right thing right the first time for our customers, employees, and partners.

An organization of leaders, all sharing the same vision and purpose, can be a powerful force. But for that new organization to work, everyone in it must be given real work to do, work that focuses on making the vision and purpose real—in short, that focuses on reengineering. What are we in business for? those leaders must ask. Who are we in business for? At CIGNA, as it mobilized for change, the focus would be on its newly discovered customer, the individual health care consumer. Everything else could be stripped away.

Lawrence English: I spent the first several weeks of my tenure going out and talking to customers, visiting our sales and claims offices, and health plan providers, and I realized this organization had far too many layers. There were three regional presidents, very highly compensated. They had their own sales, underwriting, and financial departments and their own health plan operations. Reporting to them were the area VPs. Reporting to them, in some cases, were sub-regional managers and then you got down to the field level—where the work got done.

By regionalizing we had given away all of the economies of scale, and all the opportunities to export best practices from one health plan to another. Like politics, all health care is local. If you're going to run an integrated health care delivery system right, you have to be organized around your local markets; you have to be structured to serve them with an unrelenting local presence. The bottom line was that we had virtually no choice but to eliminate the regional structure if we were going to capture the inherent competitive advantages we still had.

The impact of dismantling and rebuilding our infrastructure was as traumatic as any event I've been through. You're running a huge enterprise; you have millions of customers; you're processing millions of transactions daily. None of that stops while you make very dramatic change.

But, given what we had to do—moving from meeting the needs of corporate customers to becoming an integrated health care deliverer—we couldn't possibly have acted incrementally. I would wager that it was as major a shift in focus and structure as made by any other firm over the course of the last 10 years. No one in that situation believes incremental change will ensure your survival.

Today, we have an organization of general managers in each of our markets who are responsible for those markets. These are people who would have been three or four layers down in the old organization.

Michael A. Stocker, president, CIGNA Healthplan: It takes a lot of local talent because each market is different. You can't just go to a site and say, "Do these 10 things," and come back in six months to see if they've been done. General managers must exercise a lot of day-to-day judgment calls: how do you present the network configuration to your customers, and so on. People who are good at this combine sales, financial, and health plan administrative skills.

If you think of our industry, it has been a kind of jumbling together of very different cultures and traditions—insurance people, physicians, hospital staffs, and others. We are creating managers who are generalists, who see the whole picture, know how to run a hospital, are experienced in the complexities of different markets, and can now manage delivery systems with all the legal, financial, accounting, and quality control resources that the central organization supplies.

Mobilizing must never stop. Change will continue to be the one constant; for reengineering to live, the company needs to be continually reinfused with mission and purpose. As a consequence, managers must continually walk in their marketplace, asking the questions that began the mobilization process.

Lawrence English: People have a hard time finding me in my office. Today I'm in Philadelphia, yesterday I spoke by phone hook-up to over 100 provider-relations people in Nashville, over the weekend I was in Florida, and I was in California last week. And I'm not the only one doing this. Each of my senior managers has been in our local markets with the same story.

It's trite, but there's no getting away from the fact that the best leaders are the best communicators. You have to be in front of your employees with a consistent, forcefully told story that they understand, accept, and act upon.

When I talk to folks I always begin with what it is we are trying to do, how important our mission is to society, and how lucky we are to have this opportunity. Regardless of what kind of legislative solution is eventually proposed, we have an extraordinary opportunity right now to demonstrate that we as an industry and we as a company can restructure the way health care is delivered, producing a higher quality result at a lower cost. If we do that we will really succeed as an enterprise. People relate to that.

Mobilization begins at the top, with a vision and a business idea, but the energy comes from pushing authority and accountability down to where the action is.

Jim Olson, general manager, Video Communications Division, Hewlett-Packard: My boss had a vision of changing the oldest division of HP into a new business with much higher growth opportunities—video. He asked me to put together a business plan with the current team there and transform the division.

The division made microwave instrumentation, but sales were declining and profits too. I hired a new staff to help me formulate a new business plan, each member having the expertise we needed—R&D, marketing, manufacturing, personnel, and finance. I interviewed about 100 people in order to hire five (all came from inside the company), and over a period of time we developed a very exciting plan that centers on video servers for two markets, the broadcast market and the broad-band video-on-demand market.

There is almost no relationship between the old division and what we have now. We basically reengineered the whole place. We changed the name of it, changed the location, we sell to customers who have no relationship to the old ones.

Radical change is sometimes, in some ways, the easiest to accomplish. Making a clean break with the past sends a mobilizing jolt of energy through the company, but only when people are given some sense of control over what happens next.

Jim Olson: It was something we'd never done at HP before—taken an old division and reengineered it quite this drastically. Our traditional way of going into a new business is to ask the division that's most closely affiliated with that business's market to slowly begin to invest in it. In this case, we made a conscious effort to move quickly, to take everything a division was doing and put it someplace else and throw lots of people at the new product area. We picked the microwave division mostly because a number of top people were leaving. That gave me, as the new general manager of the division, a tremendous freedom. We took our R&D and our marketing engineers and we rechanneled their tremendous talents into this new marketplace. We didn't do any formal educating, but we provided our engineers with a lot of airline tickets and tickets to trade shows and books to learn the new customers, the new technology, which they picked up fairly readily.

We did develop a process that I call judgment-based leadership, which empowers people to make decisions very quickly and pretty much on their own. (Every product we've brought to market has been created in less than nine months and there have been about 20 of them.) We stripped away a lot of the traditional bureaucracy that creeps into large divisions and companies.

Sink-or-swim is no more a sound policy in management than it is in the swimming pool. Water-wings are no good, either, just another form of command-and-control. The best policy is clear, measurable guidelines—swimming lessons, if you will.

Jim Olson: We have a set of four success factors that we borrowed from our very successful printer group that we try to get every manager in the place to think about in considering a course of action. The first asks whether the action takes advantage of emerging technology trends and customer needs in the video market products. Any activity in the division that would help do that, and make us first in the marketplace with a new product, we pretty much sanction.

The second key success factor is to have the lowest cost structure in the industry that we were entering. Any decisions within the division that would help lower the cost structure were listened to very carefully and very quickly. For instance, we downsized the division by 55 percent, a decision made less painful by the fact we don't lay people off or fire them at HP; we find other jobs for them. We also decided to move the division about 15 miles south to Santa Clara, thereby saving HP $2 million a year in lease expenses, and saving our own division another $2 million a year by sharing services with another division that we were going to be co-located with. We made that decision within two weeks and moved the division nine months later to the day.

The third key success factor we adopted was to minimize bureaucracy, and to make decisions and centralize activity at the lowest possible level in the organization. We have really stripped bureaucracy out of the place. If a person had a good idea, we let them carry it through all the way to the handshake with the technology partner or key customer.

The fourth key success factor is having key partners in the business—technology partners and customer partners. Partners with long staying power.

One thing Emersonian thinking sometimes forgets, at its peril: that the past, paradoxically, may also be a place to go for "new" ideas. This is especially true if there is a sound underlying culture.

Jim Olson: Our CEO, Lew Platt, talks a lot about balancing continuity and change. The change part was the new leadership practices that I described, the four key success factors. We decided to apply start-up management practices inside our division within a 55-year-old company. That is the change part, and I think it's what really helped us be successful.

The continuity part was going back to the HP Way. The HP Way is really our core values, our company culture based on trust and respect for individuals. It's about empowering people at the lowest level of the organization to run with their ideas. That freedom fosters a lot of creativity and enthusiasm.

I am often asked how we changed the culture of HP within our division. The answer is we didn't. We really went back to the core culture and emphasized it more. People were familiar with the HP Way, but the division had lost sight of it. It had gotten bogged down in bureaucracy and bigness. The people in the division welcomed a return to the HP Way. A potential obstacle was that the average length of service in the division was over 15 years, which was the longest in the company. We turned that to our advantage. These people knew the HP Way from years earlier. They knew it worked. We just reinforced it.

Guidelines are not enough. The reengineering manager thinks of his job, one part of it anyway, as being a constant conversation with his people.

Jim Olson: Mostly we led by example. We just started giving out assignments and trusting people to carry them through, as opposed to going around giving speeches. Not that we neglected the communication side. I still do a monthly coffee talk. We get all the employees in the same room and tell them what is going on and what our new vision is. We did that from the day I walked in the door. We want to communicate the sense of adventure—the journey we're all taking together. We also have a hotline, a voice mailbox people can call to hear a message from me. I leave a different message every week about how we're doing. People can leave messages and suggestions. Every other week we have breakfasts with small groups—10–15 employees— to discuss what we're doing and solicit their input.

Sink-or-swim is a lousy way to grant people authority and autonomy, but it is the way of the marketplace, and it does no harm for managers to remind the company of this hard truth.

Jim Olson: There was also a survival mentality that we built into the division. We made it clear to people that it wasn't an entitlement atmosphere. It was an earning one and we were either going to succeed in this new mission or we were going to have to place a lot more people, including myself, in new jobs. We didn't threaten people, but we made it clear that it was succeed or drown. I think that helped fire people up.

Numbers give us a sense of security. Like a course on a navigational chart, they tell us where we've come from and where we're going.

Jim Olson: I am not a big believer in visions, but when you drag people through this type of change you need one. We keep it simple. We were going to shrink the division by 65 percent the first year by giving away a lot of products to the other divisions. We were becoming smaller in a company where you get points by getting bigger. So vision number one became: Grow the place to the size it was before we started this transformation by 1997. It turns out we are going to beat that all to hell. Vision number two: To become a model for leading HP into this new business and creating a multi-billion-dollar market by the year 2000. We're going to beat that too. There are now many divisions involved in the video business in HP. We started as the point division, but today we are just one of many divisions focusing resources on the vast opportunities in the video and multi-media explosion.

Not many companies have the luxury of knowing the exact hour when the clock will run out on their era of Smooth Sailing. The NutraSweet Company did have that luxury. It was common knowledge that their patent expired on December 14, 1992. So, long before then, top managment began mobilizing the company

to compete in what for them would be novel circumstances: a
free market, where customers had someplace else to go.

Michael Vinitsky, senior director of Organization of Effectiveness, NutraSweet: It was clear that we were going to have a
dramatic culture change. Things would have to be done differently—to maintain the sweetener business we'd have to become
a much broader food ingredient company. But we didn't know
how to change, or what the changes should look like, and there
was a good deal of apprehension that we wouldn't be successful
in meeting the stiff competition.

We knew that we would need to be much more externally
focused. With the expiration of our patent, suddenly people had
the option to go elsewhere to get our ingredient.

So we had to build stronger relationships with our customers, relationships based on value. We had to demonstrate
that the price they were paying was worth it. We had to get people to understand how to listen, talk, and think from a customer's point of view.

This was the purpose of one of our major initiatives, a program we called the High Performance People Development Initiative. During the first year we recruited about 100 people from
across the company, including the VP and director level, to participate. People would take on a work-related project—it had to
be one that challenged and stretched them, that required them to
work with other people to get results. For example, one salesperson took on trying to get the so-called "New Age" beverage people to use our product. She was successful and generated a significant volume of sales, as well as breaking into a new category
for the company.

As another example, someone in the sales group championed
custom packaging. NutraSweet had been sold to customers primarily in 55-pound drums. This person took on the intricacies
of what it would take to get custom packaging for different customer needs. That may not sound like a big deal, but coming
from the mindset that we were in, it required a lot of courage
and risk taking and working with delicate internal relationships.

The initiative project was part of their job. They had to go to
their manager and say, "I want to participate in this program. It

will cost a certain amount of money and in return I promise to demonstrate the following results." The manager would say yes or no. We started at the higher levels first. The second year we added 50 more participants. We are trying to build a high performance culture, a large network of people across our company who act and think in dramatically different ways than they did before.

If you are going to have an external customer focus and if your whole business strategy is based on providing value added services to your customers, so you can command a premium price, you have to have your internal resources allocated, coordinated, and integrated on the most important customer initiatives. So you need to have R&D, marketing, HR, finance, legal, all of those people working together and supporting the lead people, who are the sales account people. You can't have a functional focus, with people saying, "I'm in R&D; I do the things that R&D people do." No. We are all in this to build a sustained competitive advantage. You are not here solely to perform your function. You are here to add value.

A lot of the material you read in the literature about change leads you to believe that you have to take these bureaucracies and shake them up. That has never been the dilemma at NutraSweet. The dilemma with us has been integrating and coordinating separate factions.

You have to have a critical mass of people who believe in the future of the company and who continually ask what they can do to make a difference. And you have to reward them financially and non-financially. The challenge is to get a large group of people energized and focused—and then keep them that way.

One reason that reengineering is a radical undertaking is that once you've begun, there is literally no containing it. One thing, as they say, leads to another—or it had better, lest the whole endeavor collapse.

Michael Vinitsky: Take the people who monitor our complicated chemical processes. They control how efficiently the stuff is put out. But you have to show them how what they do impacts business outcomes.

One of the means for getting this across involves implementing self-managed work teams, where you take groups of people and give them more responsibility. You take out the supervisor level of management and give people more autonomy in terms not only of managing themselves, but of managing the work process. But to do that you have to give people increased technical skills, increased problem solving skills, and increased interpersonal skills. So it required a major investment in the training and development of people across the plant.

Some of the operators sit in a room and observe a computerized display of how the process is working. They could stop the process, or make some minor modifications if the process was outside some of the parameters. It was felt that if the people understood more about the principles behind the chemical process and had better problem solving skills they could reduce waste, intervene more quickly, and not have to rely on as many technical experts to make decisions. It was trying to provide a smaller group of people with a larger range of skills and knowledge, which is the whole concept of self-managing work teams. Give them the accountability so when something goes wrong, rather than calling the supervisor, they would have the skill, knowledge, and judgment to intervene themselves.

People claim that significant change requires commitment from the top. True, the top is necessary, but it's not enough. No CEO can do this alone. You need to have a critical mass of people in the company at both upper and middle levels who are really committed to making change happen and are in it for the long haul. That critical mass has to be consistent in their actions; they all have to be speaking the same language. They also have to continually enroll and encourage others to come on board, making them feel wanted, needed, an important part of the company's future.

You can see how these three companies either had an underlying culture that supported the changes, or recognized the need to adjust their culture in order to reengineer. In the next chapter I will explore in greater depth this question of culture and behavior, a question that reengineers must continuously live.

CHAPTER 6

WHAT KIND OF CULTURE DO WE WANT?

*I've noticed a curious thing on my travels among managers
over the last year or so. People now seem to get just as
excited about coming up with corporate values statements
as they did about designing organization charts.
But it's really not so curious, is it?
Everything we've learned about reengineering drives toward
one solid conclusion: The rules of governance (and self-
governance) for effective business enterprises today are
being determined by their culture, not their organizational
structure.*

In the days of Smooth Sailing, corporate culture was dictated by
two factors: the hierarchical structure that corporations inherited, and the modern myth of the organizational "machine." The
culture dictated by these factors was basically one of obedience—

to the imperatives of a chain of *command*, and to the demands of a highly *controlled* task.

In the Rough Weather we're sailing in today, a culture of obedience is still called for, but the authority we must obey is totally different. It is no longer anything so simple, stable, and rational as a hierarchy of corporate powers or the specifics of a job description. The new authority lives in our markets and usually appears in the form of our customers. You must have a culture that encourages qualities like relentless pursuit (to match our customers' elusiveness), bottomless resources of imagination (to create needs our customers may not know they have), and both smooth teamwork and individual autonomy (to match their demanding standards). You cannot have a culture of obedience to chains of command and the job slot. It just won't work. The markets will punish you for it.

Let's be clear what this shift does *not* mean, however.

It doesn't mean that hierarchical chains of command or detailed job descriptions are completely vanishing from corporate life. There are some enterprises (small service companies, perhaps) whose goods or services are produced and brought to market by so few people that no arrangements have to be made to coordinate the work of production and marketing. In such an enterprise, all of the players can fit into a room (real or virtual) to make decisions together. Anything larger, more dispersed, or more work specialized usually requires an "elevated" or "centralized" platform from which it's possible to see what's going on. Somebody has to answer for the coordination of the whole enterprise. Hierarchy grows out of that brute fact, as does the "job slot."

But nothing else that we normally associate with hierarchies and job slots needs to grow out of that fact. Thick layers of bureaucracy, airtight segmentation of functions, social inequalities are all strictly optional—and ruinous. Organizations that carry such burdens, as I've seen again and again, simply cannot compete in truly free, competitive markets. They are not adept enough, quick enough, imaginative enough, high-spirited enough, or, in the end, rich enough to win the support of customers.

But all those layers of bureaucracy and narrow job descriptions cannot merely be jettisoned. This stuff is the life of a corporation. Where it exists, a hierarchical, bureaucratic structure doesn't simply support an organization, like the girders in a skyscraper. It is the armature of our deepest on-the-job feelings and attachments as well. Just think, for example, how hierarchy structures what is for many of us our most creative impulse, our ambition. Not everyone can be an entrepreneur, determined to make something out of nothing. Most of us, if we want to rise in the world, must have something to *climb*. Without a hierarchy (or with a very flat one), how are ambitious people going to measure their climb? How do you go up a ladder with only a few rungs—two at the bottom, say, and two at the top; with two more off to the side somewhere, in R&D? The fact is, it may not be possible, during long periods of our working lives in the reengineered corporation, to speak of "rising in the world" at all.

In short, reducing hierarchy, bureaucracy, and the rest of it is not just a matter of rearranging the furniture to face our customers and markets. It is a matter of rearranging the quality of people's attachments—to their work and to each other. These are *cultural* matters, and they define the second great "living question" for managers today: how to change our business's culture, and in what way.

The new enthusiasm for drawing up values statements comes from the need to answer that question effectively. "The future," Robert Hall, author of *The Soul of the Enterprise*: *Creating a Dynamic Vision for American Manufacturing*, tells us, "belongs to those [managers] who can *frequently* reorganize *high-morale* teams around the needs of *changing* processes." If that's true, and it is, then values become the most important structural elements in the enterprise. Why? Values are the link between emotion and behavior, the connection between what we feel and what we do. Values instruct our feelings so that we don't always have to pause and think before we act on them. Note the terrific strain between the two imperatives of Hall's remark—high morale and frequent changes. Keeping our spirits up in the midst of continuous change is difficult—unless, as Mark DeMichele of

Arizona Public Service reminded us in Chapter 4, we are blessed with the appropriate values. With everything changing around us, we need something unchanging—north stars or touchstones, commandments, slogans, or aphorisms—to hang on to, to find our bearings with, and to steady our nerves. Values are our moral navigational devices.

They are business navigational devices as well. As hierarchies flatten, and power, control, and responsibility get pushed out from HQ to the trenches, from staff to line, we need to know that the people "out there" will do the right thing at the moment of truth. The reverse is equally true: The people out there, customers as well as employees, need to know that the folks back at HQ will also do the right thing. At the time of the Tylenol crisis, for example, I remember Jim Burke, then chairman of Johnson & Johnson, saying that there was never any question, given the company's strong values, but that all Tylenol capsules would be removed from shelves and warehouses. The cost to the company ran to millions of dollars, but the benefit was literally beyond price. That's *where* values are, at the crossroads between decency and sound profit, and that's where a culture must be built.

WHAT VALUES?

So let's get down to it—what kind of values do we want, what kind of culture?

I wish there was a simple answer to this question, but there's not. Values take their shape and substance from many sources—from the "real" business the business is in (are we a bookstore or a theater?); from the realm of metaphors (are we a track team or a basketball team?); from the political and social ideals of the company's native land (are we protecting jobs or free markets?); from the individual beliefs of the people in the company. These sources are so different, and mix so differently in different corporations, that it is hopeless to expect a single statement of values that could fit all companies.

Nevertheless, I have participated in and observed reengineering projects in hundreds of corporations, and I've noticed striking similarities in the values and behaviors promoted by their different cultures. What's emerging, I would argue, is a broad, humanly satisfying culture of what I call willingness, the willingness, specifically . . .

1. To perform up to the highest measure of competence, always.
2. To take initiatives and risks.
3. To adapt to change.
4. To make decisions.
5. To work cooperatively as a team.
6. To be open, especially with information, knowledge, and news of forthcoming or actual "problems."
7. To trust, and be trustworthy.
8. To respect others (customers, suppliers, and colleagues) and oneself.
9. To answer for our actions, to accept responsibility.
10. To judge and be judged, reward and be rewarded, on the basis of our performance.

The first thing to notice about this list is that the items fall neatly into two groups. The first five represent *work values*, meaning that they're particularly appropriate to the work setting, to the job and how it is performed. The second five are human virtues, pure and simple, appropriate to living and working fruitfully in a larger, orderly society. Openness, trust and trustworthiness, self-respect and mutual respect, cooperativeness, accountability, even the willingness to judge and be judged, reward and be rewarded—these *social values* are esteemed by most of the larger cultures in the developed world, and are encouraged (or should be) by most of our parents, teachers, friends, and fellow citizens.

Not that managers can count on finding these virtues in the corporation, unfortunately. Even the family, America's most powerful agent of cultural instruction, is having a desperately hard time teaching our children so much as the rudiments of self-governance. But even if all our sons and daughters could be brought up living by the Boy and Girl Scout Handbooks, we would still need to foster a fitting corporate culture to support them as adults in their socially virtuous ways.

Why? Look again at our values of a culture of willingness and note the inevitable tension. The first asks our people always to perform to their highest measure, while the tenth asks them to judge and be judged, reward and be rewarded, accordingly. It is a hard fact of corporate life that the willingness to judge and be judged on the basis of performance puts a strain on the virtues of trust, respect, and team-playing. Judgments and rewards are invidious, especially within a closed, stressful environment. They are, in fact, meant to be invidious. They count on the nearly universal human desire for approval to induce us to provide better and better performances—better and better, that is, as judged and rewarded by standards against which other people besides ourselves are also being judged and rewarded. Inevitably, comparisons will be made; inevitably, they will be painful to some, delightful to others; inevitably, therefore, they will arouse some degree of envy, discord, self-regarding fear, even malice.

That's where the culture comes in, or should. Unless it is *strongly* supportive of trust, respect, and teamwork, these social values will become purely personal and private, disappearing underground.

A CASE OF BAD VALUES

That's what happened, evidently, at a financial services company that I'll call Company ABC. In the 1950s and 1960s, Company ABC put in world-class performances in its field. But growth began to stall in the 1970s, then margins began to contract. By 1988, the company's president, Bill X, concluded that the trouble was in their marketing strategy: "Mass" was out, the customer was in. Bill X ordered up a new marketing strategy, carefully articulating his new customer-driven vision of the business. But nothing changed.

So Bill X ordered up what's known as a "cultural audit"—a

deep sounding of a company's actual as opposed to professed values.

The results, for an outfit that was staking its future on customer service, were disturbing. The audit uncovered six rules, or operating assumptions, that seemed to be guiding the conduct of Company ABC employees.

The first assumption was: *Only your friends are trustworthy.* People had close ties with each other at Company ABC, but they were personal ties, not collegial ones. They had nothing to do with the work setting per se, only with self-protection in an atmosphere of rampant mistrust. Ideas were stolen, or thought to be stolen, and thieves got promoted; thus management was seen to be unjust. At the same time, top-down information was distributed only on the strictest "need-to-know" basis; therefore management was seen to be indifferent or disdainful. Fear spread like a virus. Subordinates hoarded ideas and information themselves, the better to hold on to what little status and authority they had. Willingness to change, to innovate, to turn in optimal performances, never mind our so-called social virtues—none of these flourished at Company ABC, except for underground purposes.

The second assumption was: *Employees are overhead, not assets.* This was an unavoidable conclusion that employees drew from what they saw as facts: the inadequate investment in learning, training, and development; the "glass ceiling" for women; the absence of promotions from within to senior management. Whether these were indeed facts or warped perceptions didn't matter: Employees felt that they were not treated with respect. Lack of respect, we reengineering practitioners agree, may be the most devastating managerial "sin." Its impact goes straight to the bottom line, in lackluster performances and contagiously low spirits.

The third assumption was: *Disagreement is bad.* Disagreement is always a risky business, whether it's with your immediate boss, your team, or the company culture. Disagreement invites conflict; conflict (often) creates winners and losers; and it's not pleasant to lose. At Company ABC, people had institutionalized this normal fear of disagreement. The bywords there were: "To get along, go along," "The boss is always right," etc. This is disastrous. A culture that squashes disagreement is a culture doomed to stagnate, because change always begins with disagreement. Besides, disagreement can never be squashed entirely. It gets repressed, to emerge later as a pervasive sense of injustice, followed by apathy, resentment, and even sabotage.

The fourth assumption was: *Internal rivalries are healthy*. This cultural assumption, based on the old adversarial ethic, is too deeply flawed to work today. Its competitive spirit fosters a spirit of introspective self-regard—Me-Me-ism—that can end up totally *dis*regarding the company's actual competition (its commercial rivals). At Company ABC, for example, the cultural audit found that marketing departments were vying with each other to attract customers. This seemed appropriate by the old "Come out fighting, and may the best person win" ethic. But it was totally counterproductive. Customers were driven away by the fact that one Company ABC unit could not seem to coordinate its service with another ABC unit that was ostensibly operating out of the same playbook. Moreover, departments internally were jealous, perhaps even deceitful, struggling over the available resources they needed to compete. This might have been tolerable in a Smooth Sailing business with an internal market and limitless resources, but few such businesses exist today.

The fifth rule was: *Excellent performance is not a core value*. The cultural audit revealed a widespread conviction that it wasn't what you accomplished but how busy you looked that mattered. Quantity, not quality of work, was prized; favoritism was epidemic ("It's not what you do, it's who you work for"); and a staggering three-quarters of the workforce assumed that legitimate qualifications didn't matter when people got promoted. This assumption fed back into all the others: personal not collegial alliances, mistrust, disrespect, repression, and so forth. It also spewed an emotional pollutant all its own. Confused and frustrated, employees worried constantly about their own job security, since there were no clear guidelines on what kind of performance assured their worth to the company.

The sixth assumption was, operationally, the most ruinous: *The customer is incidental.* Note that all the preceding assumptions have the effect of turning everyone *inward*, on themselves or on their immediate circle of friends. Neglect of the customer follows as the night the day. At Company ABC, this neglect was symbolized by the piles and piles of untargeted, redundant mailings that were sent out to potential customers. The cultural atmosphere was so toxic with internal tension and anxiety that no one was *minding* the store.

BEWARE: WEEDS PUSH OUT FLOWERS

I'm happy to report that Company ABC has now pulled itself together, thanks to a massive reengineering of work processes *and* management—including, above all, management values and culture. But the managers of ABC would do well to remember two vital points: Its new culture will have to be very strong to overcome the old one, and it will have to remain strong to keep the old one from coming back.

The reason is simple: There's a kind of law of corporate cultures, that bad values tend to drive out good ones, first the good social values, then the good work values. Why this should be so has something to do, again, with the stresses and strains produced by our First and Tenth willingnesses. But mostly it has to do with the fact that good cultures require hard work to establish and maintain, while bad cultures do not. Flourishing gardens need careful planting, fertilizing, and weeding—in a word, *cultivating.* Weedy gardens are "low-maintenance"; they "go of themselves," as (by no coincidence) we said of the machine-like corporation.

Cultures that squash disagreement, for example, are insidiously easy to launch, and the culprit is almost always at the enterprise manager level. No one likes to be disagreed with, but equally, no one likes to admit it, especially someone with the high stakes in being *right* that top managers have. Thus the stage is set for a drama of denial: "Go ahead—disagree with me," the traditional boss's voice says. "And suffer the consequences," his face and body language insist. The loser in *this* conflict, needless to say, is the enterprise.

Managers, once again, have to change. They have to get out in the open, and open themselves to the possibility of being wrong. Surrendering the attitude of command and no longer worrying about loss of control are essential first steps in this openness. No one will fault you for wrongheadedness if you approach problems with the easy, self-confident assumption that you, and you alone, are not the only person who can come up with the right answer.

Managers face the same challenge with cultures that foster internal rivalries. That's because we (Americans especially) truly believe in the adversarial ethic of "Come out fighting, may the best person win." We believe in it because it works so well in so many arenas (think of that word *arena* for a minute)—courtrooms, politics, markets, and so forth. Thus the CEO often cannot help letting his or her junior officers know that it's all right if they compete among themselves for the CEO's approval. Thus, too, the division chief applauds "a little healthy competition" among his or her teams. It will all work out for the best. And so it might, in the best of all possible worlds. But we do not work in such a world, not any longer. The wind has shifted, the revolution is upon us, and we cannot afford the waste of energies and resources entailed by internal competitions. Competing for the customer is competition enough.

For managers, the moral of this story is clear—*cultivate your culture*. Only a very strong, constantly cultivated culture can prevent the weeds of mistrust, disrespect, and uncooperativeness from taking over the garden.

THE VALUE OF GOOD VALUES

Before turning to the question of how this should be done, let's look at some actual, living values statements. Of course a good values *statement* will not automatically produce a good culture (though if the first is good, there's always hope for the second, and vice versa). But I've seen firsthand that these statements are, in fact, the good fruits of good gardens.

First, here is a statement of the values nourished at Airborne Express:

Airborne is its people, teamed to satisfy the worldwide shipment and delivery needs of their customers. Every employee is an important and valued member of the Airborne team. Each strives to perform with excellence and to ensure reliable, economical, quality service. All take pride in being the industry's premier provider of customer satisfaction, in fact and by reputation. Airborne values are the foundation for the corporate drive to excel.

1. Customer satisfaction is the top priority of every employee and the purpose of every job. Cost-effective, ongoing achievement of customer satisfaction is the foundation of our business.
2. Strategies, goals, and objectives, established to ensure consistent customer satisfaction, corporate financial health, and employee development and support, are clearly defined, communicated, and understood.
3. Management believes in, promotes, and pursues excellence throughout the organization. Excellence is expected in the quality and quantity of work done by every employee in every function, both for our customers and for our fellow employees. "Doing the job right the first time" is the dominant pattern of every activity.
4. Initiative and ingenuity applied to the conduct of business and the resolution of problems are encouraged and supported throughout the organization.
5. The roles and responsibilities of every employee are clearly defined. Aggressive cooperative fulfillment on behalf of our customers and in support of Airborne strategies and goals is valued and commendable.
6. Reward structures recognize contributions to and achievement of results which enhance customer satisfaction, improve cost effectiveness, and strengthen profitability.

The results of living the Airborne values are:

- Quality service for our customers
- A rewarding work environment for our people
- Adequate return to our shareholders

Of our ten willingness behaviors, you'll notice, not one is left out of this document. But what I admire about Airborne's statement is not just its completeness, but its authenticity—it is the same quality I mentioned in Chapter 4, in relation to the statements of purpose we need to mobilize our companies for radical change. I don't know where the statement was composed, or by whom. But there's a real human voice here. You hear it, precisely, in the relentless focus on the "customer"; you hear it in the crispness of the language; and you hear it in the utterly definitive, even aggressive tone of the document. Every sentence might have begun, "Let there be no misunderstanding here . . ." If the aim of "values" is to provide some measure of certainty in an uncertain world, these values do it.

Notice, too, the constituencies to whom Airborne is addressing this statement. First and foremost, of course, is its employees: The norms have an impact directly on them. But customers and investors, too, seem invited to remember these values, and to judge the company by how well it lives up to them. As for other possible constituencies—the community, for instance—the rhetoric suggests there are none. It is focused on "employees."

If I have any criticism of the Airborne statement, it is that it leaves me with a wisp of a suspicion that even managers, somehow, are not in the intended audience. The sentences are being addressed to "all" employees, to be sure, but they leave the listener wondering whether it is perfectly clear, beyond any quibble, that management itself submits to the discipline of these values. The answer to that question, of course, will come clear only when we can see how managers actually behave.

My second example of a good values statement is addressed straightforwardly to the whole world. No constituency is left out. This is only fitting in a company as great, and greatly ambitious, as Johnson & Johnson. It also begins with the collective pronoun, "We," thus eloquently taking for granted what many companies can only strive for.

We believe our first responsibility is to the doctors, nurses and patients, to mothers and fathers and all others who use our products and services. In meeting their needs everything we do must be of high quality. We must constantly strive to reduce our costs in order to maintain reasonable prices. Customers' orders must be serviced promptly and accurately. Our suppliers and distributors must have an opportunity to make a fair profit.

We are responsible to our employees, the men and women who work with us throughout the world. Everyone must be considered as an individual. We must respect their dignity and recognize their merit. They must have a sense of security in their jobs. Compensation must be fair and adequate, and working conditions clean, orderly, and safe. We must be mindful of ways to help our employees fulfill their family responsibilities. Employees must feel free to make suggestions and complaints. There must be equal opportunity for employment, development, and advancement for those qualified. We must provide competent management, and their actions must be just and ethical.

We are responsible to the communities in which we live and work, and to the world community as well. We must be good citizens—support good works and charities and bear our fair share of taxes. We must encourage civic improvements and better health and education. We must maintain in good order the property we are privileged to use, protecting the environment and natural resources.

Our final responsibility is to our stockholders. Business must make a sound profit. We must experiment with new ideas. Research must be carried on, innovative programs developed and mistakes paid for. New equipment must be purchased, new facilities provided, and new products launched. Reserves must be created to provide for adverse times. When we operate according to these principles, the stockholders should realize a fair return.

Again, I am struck not so much by the scope of this statement, which is breathtaking, as by how wonderfully authentic it is. It is a litany of "responsibility"—the voice of an older, almost traditional capitalism, "old money" you might say. It is a voice that may be gaining strength these days, but not since the 1970s have there been a whole lot of folks who talk convincingly about "fair profit," "fair return," "sound profit," still fewer about their "fair share of taxes" or their duties to the environment and to the communities where they work. This is understandable: The competitive pressures are too great, the agony of change too relentless, profits too hard to come by, for a leisurely rhetorical consideration of our responsibilities to humankind. Customers and investors are quite enough responsibility for anyone these days.

Still, we should not be too quick to dismiss this statement as a luxury of the hereditary (and very) rich. We have to remember what business Johnson & Johnson is in. Band-Aids and baby powder, medical supplies of all kinds—they're in the *caring* business, or, we might say, the *responsibility* business. So there's a tight fit between the values of this company, the language in which it expresses them, and the way it makes its profits. There's nothing like a concord between a company's profits and its principles to strike the right—that is, the resonantly authentic—note in its language.

THE MEANING OF VALUES

Both these values statements should forcefully remind us of Mark DeMichele's remark in Chapter 4 about the manager's duty and self-interest to give our people (and ourselves) something *un*changing to hang on to in the midst of tumultuous change. As I've said before in this book, work is as meaningful an activity for us human beings as love and friendship. It is through work that we express our innate drive for competence, what noted economist Thorstein Veblen called our "instinct of craftsmanship." And as we express that instinct, we do two things. We connect with a world larger than ourselves, a world that will go on after we are dead, a bit better for our having been alive in it. In the process, through this work and these connections, we discover who we are.

Values statements, in other words, are another sort of answer to the question of Chapter 4, "What are we doing here, anyway?" Purpose (and vision) statements answer the question, at least for now, with respect to the *business* we're in. What are we up to here? What's the plan? What's in it for "them," the customers, and what's in it for "us," the corporate employees? Where do I fit into this plan? There's an underlying concern in these queries—survival. People want to know not only top management's explanation of what they think they're doing, they also want to judge for themselves what management's chances are of *succeeding* at what they're doing.

Values statements respond to the same concerns, but can, and should, go deeper. They should touch on our need for assurances that what we're doing here has some larger worldly significance than can be encompassed by this business, this job, these colleagues, and this paycheck.

It's a disturbing fact of our times that many of the other institutions in which we used to find a sense of our personal significance in a larger world—family, neighborhood, clubhouse, church, ethnic group, philanthropy, government—have lost much of their persuasive power. They don't connect us to each other as they used to, nor do they help us know ourselves as they once did. And as a result, many of us may feel more alone and more insignificant. It has come to this for many people in the West: Of all the ancient, traditional supports of humane selfhood, only work remains strong.

At this point in history, then, we managers face both a staggering responsibility and a dazzling opportunity. We are the organizers of work, and of workplaces. We can make them serve our social and psychic needs, our needs for significance, or we can allow them to stunt these needs. That's what is truly at stake in values statements—our sense of ourselves in a larger human world. The choices are ours.

YES, BUT HOW DO WE DO IT?

Making those choices, however, begs the toughest question. How do we move our companies and ourselves from the old culture—perhaps, as Company ABC's used to be, a culture of suspicion, cliquishness, and second-rate standards of performance—to a new culture that fosters the "willingness" that I've found to be common among reengineered companies?

I am tempted here to address the "top," the "center," "senior" management. There is no doubt in my mind, or in the mind of any other reengineer, that cultural change has to begin with enterprise managers. They must drive the change, in person, all the time—*teaching it, doing it, living it.* That's what it takes to bring about the revolution required here—a revolution, remember, in the way people connect to each other and to their work; a revolution in the significance of what they do and are.

And then, of course, there's the law of bad values driving out good. So managers must keep on teaching it, doing it, living it.

One of the most inspiring examples of specifically *cultural* leadership that I've found is Leslie H. Wexner, founder, chairman, and CEO of The Limited, Inc. Wexner has obviously thought long and deeply about the practicalities of cultivating his garden. Like Henry Ford, he found his business too big to be human. But unlike Ford, he did something about it other than embrace the image of the corporate "machine." His solution actually lay close at hand—in the importance of scale:

> To create a feeling of shared values, we break down our business units to a size that people can relate to. There's a perception in most of American business that bigness is better because of economies of scale. I think in terms of efficiencies of scale. I don't believe in having people pay allegiance to a monolithic $10 billion or $20 billion enterprise that employs thousands of people. It's much more effective when it's broken down to units that people can identify with and that can capture their imagination as individuals. In our company, the primary allegiance is to the operating unit, rather than The Limited, Inc. That's good for our associates, and it's good for the company.

Federalization of business monoliths, breaking them down into more or less self-governing units—down, ultimately, to the self-governing individual—is an attractive and efficient "constitution" for many corporations to adopt. But there's a serious danger in this sort of thing. We don't need current events to tell us how easy it is for federal systems, whether team-based, work process–based, or division-based, to become Balkan systems. Company ABC, with its social values driven underground, provides a good negative example. I know of another company that has become so Balkanized that its division managers speak seriously of needing a "foreign policy" to do business with one another. Some customers want to talk with a single company representative, not ten people representing ten different divisions.

But there's a way to respond to the Balkanization threat—common values, and the personal presence of the CEO as the embodiment of those values. Wexner's is that response. He personally interviews all executive hires.

That's one way he ensures that at The Limited, at least, the law of the bad driving out the good will operate in reverse:

> We want all our people to be an extension of the values of the company. They must respect those values; otherwise they'll just mouth the words. . . . New employees either accept and assimilate those values, or they sort themselves out. When I interview someone, the most important thing is that they understand how we think about things, what our values are, what the job is. I could sell them the job, and they could probably sell me themselves. But if at the end of the day they think our values and our standards are nonsense, then they'll leave.

As always with reengineering, "communicating" is the critical activity with values. We "teach it" by communicating; we "do it" by communicating; and we "live it"—that is, keep on doing it—by communicating. With values, however, there's a strict limit to the usefulness of purely verbal communications. We must also communicate by acts. If we don't, we will create the worst, and perhaps most common of all destructive corporate cultures—a culture of hypocrisy and cynicism. The verbal must be backed up by the actual; words must be followed by deeds.

Mark DeMichele spoke this need for leaders to take a "very personal responsibility" for cultural change:

> We need to epitomize the company's values, and that's why I didn't delegate that throughout the organization. I accepted that for myself, as well as our executive team. Our view is that all the

officers have to walk the talk, and so I, along with all of our officers, rolled up our sleeves. We attended every management session during [retraining], often spending 15 or 16 hours in the
course of a day . . . working alongside the employees. . . . That's
the question that we have to ask ourselves as we go though
reengineering. Are we willing, as leaders, to make that kind of
commitment?

It's a commitment, too, of more than bodily presence, more
than a willingness to "walk the talk," to "epitomize" the company's values. It's a commitment of resources, as Mark DeMichele
insists:

As leaders we have to be willing to allocate the money to make
certain that a reengineering process works in an organization.
And that, oftentimes, is very, very difficult when you're letting
people go, when you're impacting jobs. But the leader of the
organization has to be willing to fight for those resources . . .

While we should never forget that old Methodist aphorism
about walking the talk, it is important to realize how much of
the manager's task of cultivating the culture does in fact come
down to talk. This is the lesson of one of my consulting partners: "Everyday conversations—both public and private—are
the access to shifting operating states [his phrase for "changing
the culture"]." Managers must be alive to every opportunity to
reformulate, or reconceptualize, the way their people relate to
each other and to their jobs. Is the workplace still pushing up
weeds—mistrust, sabotage, resource hoarding? Managers can do
wonders by confronting the sowers of those weeds—refusing,
say, to sign off on any form of recognition that's unearned by
actual performance, then explaining precisely why they refused.
In other words, the existence of a "bad" culture can be used as a
foil, or pivot, in beginning the creation of a new and better culture.

There's a well-known story about Xerox that illustrates what
walking the talk can do. The transformation of the company
began, so the story goes, at an annual shareholders meeting in

1981. Xerox had recently halted production of a notoriously unreliable new copier, the 3300, which was supposed to be the answer to low-cost Japanese competitors. When the then-CEO, David Kearns, opened the meeting for questions, a Xerox assembly-line worker named Frank Enos stepped up to the microphone. In a booming voice, Enos told his CEO, "We all knew the 3300 was a piece of junk. We could have told you. Why didn't you ask us?" Kearns set about finding the answer, and changed the culture as a result. When the U.S. Department of Commerce awarded Xerox a Baldrige Quality Award in 1989, Kearns invited Frank Enos to the ceremony in Washington.

That's merely "symbolic" talk, it might be said, little more than a nice gesture. But symbols and gestures are vital tools in the managerial shop, and Xerox management hardly stops there. They talk "real" talk, repeatedly. Every year at the end of January, Paul Allaire, who succeeded Kearns as chairman and CEO in 1991, conducts a two-hour broadcast called "Focus," which includes a segment of call-in questions. But "Focus" is the second step in the company's annual verbal blitz. The first is a meeting between Allaire and Xerox's top 150 managers at the company's Stamford, Connecticut, headquarters, just before the "Focus" broadcast. The blitz continues after the broadcast as Allaire goes on the road to meet with groups of managers in about a dozen Xerox offices. Also, whenever he travels, Allaire meets with small groups of rank-and-file employees (potential Frank Enoses, presumably) for roundtable discussions. Employees also get a chance to size up their CEO every quarter on another call-in show, two hours long, called "Ask Your CEO." If Allaire doesn't get to a question on the show, his office mails a response.

WHEN SENIOR MANAGERS BALK

More often than I wish, on my visits to companies, someone asks whether it's possible to do reengineering in a culture that's not open to change. I've seen the effects of such cultures myself, and they are unforgettable. One senior manager, during a meeting with the change team, expressed his hostility, or anxiety, by opening his briefcase and reading his mail. Another, I remember, began reading his newspaper. Several have walked out of the room, announcing they have more important things to do.

The culture behind this sort of behavior is almost invariably an outgrowth of a hierarchical structure, an arrangement that's Taylor-made, so to speak, for the encouragement of a command-and-control style of management, and for more or less conscious expectations of machine-like responsiveness in the organization. Because such organizations are expressly designed to wipe out all possibility of human error, loss, or whatever, they also tend to suppress all possibility of human imagination, initiative, decisiveness, dissent, individual responsibility, or real teamwork.

It may seem incredible to an outsider, a reengineer, say, that people will actually fight to conserve such a cultural setting for their working lives. But of course they do. It is what they know, a safe harbor in a dark and stormy time—why should they risk setting sail for distant and unknown ports? Why should they want to change?

Two circumstances can reinforce this stubborn and fearful conservatism. One, of course, is success. In a business that's been successful for a good long time, senior management can always trot out the old cliché, "If it ain't broke, don't fix it," which makes them sound tough while acting timorous. The other, equally obvious, is a traditionally protected market such as many utilities once enjoyed.

But let's go back to the original question: Is there any reason to hope for change when the culture of the company, reinforced by senior management, is unwilling, or downright hostile? For real change, change across organizational boundaries, change that actually makes a difference in the way people work and manage work—and makes a difference, too, in the success of the business—the answer is no. There is always the possible change in the CEO (for better, of course); or a visible radical change in the marketplace; or actual disaster that forces senior management to change its position. From time to time, the board or investors will revolt, but by then, it's often too late. My advice to those of you who may be caught within such an environment is to keep trying to convince senior management of the business case for change. Sometimes, armed with enough data suggesting impending disaster, you can find an opening at the top—one senior manager to champion the case for change. That's often all it takes to begin the process.

BEWARE OF BANALITY

The greatest enemy of a new, reengineered culture of willingness is the old culture of cynicism, self-regarding fear, and mistrust. It is always there, like the seeds of weeds, waiting to infest the place again. But there is a second great enemy of the new culture, almost as invidious—banality.

Not that people will grow disaffected by the *values* of the new culture. Those ten underlying values of social and work behavior can never wear out so long as people work, and work cooperatively. Nevertheless, there is a sort of iron law that dictates that the *expression*, the *rhetoric*, the *statements* of values do wear out. People get tired of hearing the same old phrases, with the same old tone of aggressive urgency, in the same old forums. It's not that they cynically dismiss them, it's simply that they cannot any longer hear them. Even in dealing with what passes for eternal verities in the business world, change is the rule. Managers have to fight banality every day, primarily by actually acting on the values and expressions they talk about so often. But they also have to keep the language they use fresh to keep its meaning alive.

CHAPTER 7

CASES IN POINT—WHAT WE WANTED

Identifying the values that define a culture of
reengineering—that is, a culture that willingly embraces the
need for constant change—is only a necessary first step.
To make those values and that culture thrive within your
corporate community, and to remove all the "weeds,"
requires teaching, living, and doing at all levels of the
organization at all times.

A culture, as we have seen, can neither be simply proclaimed nor easily manipulated. The good news is that when you clear away the weeds of bad behavior, you often find a set of values that once guided a company and to which people still aspire. In most cases, however, it will be necessary to update those values, to put them in sync with changing times. For example, what "respect for the individual" meant at IBM during the years when "jobs for life" was the norm is certainly different than what "respect for the individual" means at the IBM of today. There is still an aspiration on the part of IBMers to live by that "respect for the individual" credo, but in terms that better fit the conditions (expressed or implied) we now have about continued employment.

But whether you are just weeding out bad behavior, making your company's values more contemporary, or actually attempting more radical cultural change, here are five not-so-easy steps to move you toward your objective. (Please note that I specifically use the language "move you toward," because every statement of a company's values, beliefs, or "willingness" that I have seen is an aspiration—no company is ever quite where it wants to be in terms of actual behavior. That's why you'll be constantly living this question of culture.)

1. Determine what values are deeply shared by people in the company. There are probably just a few of them, five or six at most. Don't trust a published values statement; look at how people actually behave to see the real values they share.

2. Assess what bad behavior may have driven out the good. Where are the weeds?

3. Articulate what values and behaviors you must move toward. These will be determined by what the reengineered work and your markets require, together with your aspirations as a community of people.

4. Examine your management processes. Do they support your aspirations for values and behavior, or do they contradict them? (You'll learn more about what these management processes are in the next chapter.)

5. Start teaching, doing, and living the values you want to define your culture.

Let's look now and see what we can learn from people who are actually doing this teaching, doing, and living.

TEACHING

To change the behavior of a community of people, a common goal must be clearly expressed.

Leon Royer, executive director of Organizational Learning Services, 3M: When I took over the electronics department, it was losing money and morale was low. The employees' sense of teamwork was crumbling. When things aren't going well, people tend to break down into what I call granular formats, like grains of sand; there's no connective material binding them together. They become isolated, their focus narrows down to just their own job, and they lose sight of the big picture.

The first thing I did was concentrate on turning those 100 employees into a team. The linchpin for a strong team structure is a sense of shared destiny. So I set out to get everyone focused on the same goal, which was to "delight the customer!" We repeated over and over again: "The customer gives meaning and purpose to our jobs!"

It took some time to pull everyone's focus onto the big picture, the common goal. But once I was able to instill that message of a shared destiny, the sense of teamwork followed naturally.

Teaching must be both formal and informal. But formal "interventions" are often required as external changes raise new, and often troubling, challenges to a large organization's culture.

Armando Flores, vice president of Human Resources, Arizona Public Service: Cultural concepts have a tremendous impact on every employee. In order to develop strategies for dealing with these cultural issues, we hold weeklong sessions in a hotel for a hundred employees at a time.

For example, we did a session on the issue of what we call the new workforce paradigm: recognizing that companies can no longer guarantee lifelong employment in exchange for loyalty. The question becomes: What then is the new employer/employee at Arizona Public Service? By the end of the session the employees had come up with the following "understanding": "We recognize that we can no longer be guaranteed lifelong employment; however, we do understand that if we add value to the company through our own performance and the company is successful in its business, we will be rewarded fairly, work in a safe and healthy environment, and be able to pursue personal and professional development opportunities."

We had another session to deal with the topic of diversity. Our objective is to celebrate the whole concept of cultural diversity, and to take advantage of its benefits so dramatically that we can be a model for other companies to follow.

We also held a session on the "integrated person," dealing with the issue of maximizing human potential. Most people operate at about 75 percent of their true potential. If a company can find a way to help people identify and use their untapped potential, that additional productivity is going to be reflected not only in the bottom line but in their personal lives.

We're looking for what we call "breakthrough concepts" to come out of these sessions. The hundred people go to the hotel, stay there, and meet every day in a conference room.

People are allowed to leave at night if they have a need. A tenet of our culture is to help people balance their work and personal lives, and we would be going against that if we didn't allow people to go home. But generally we like them to stay because the sessions often go until 10 P.M. The idea is to get everybody stimulated about the topic and working together.

Something wonderful happens at these sessions. The participants become a cohesive group, a real bonding takes place over those five days. There are no formalities, no titles, everybody has an equal voice. There are charts all over the walls. There are videos. People dress in shorts and T-shirts.

The session starts with a case for action and a lot of strategy-based brainstorming around specific issues, but then goes past the brainstorming to actually generate specific ideas we call deliverables. On Friday, graduation day, each group presents their ideas to company visitors and to our officers. It's not uncommon for people to be up until 4 A.M. on Thursday night putting finishing touches on their presentations.

Once the deliverables are accepted there is an implementation calendar developed so they can become part of the operational mainstream.

There is great power in using metaphors to teach culture—a power that is compounded when teaching stresses the alignment process of personal and company values.

Bob O'Neal, senior manager, Universal Card University, AT&T Universal Card Services: After having successfully completed our rigorous hiring process, employees are ready for Passport to Excellence, a two-day, experientially based program about our culture, vision, and values. Passport to Excellence is not a training session. There is no test at the end. It's an opportunity for employees to examine who they are, to compare their goals with our company mission, and to explore what will make them successful within the company.

People are divided into table groups, and we begin with icebreaking exercises, to get them warmed up. Although they'll be working in these table teams, they'll also work as an entire classroom group.

The metaphor we use for Passport to Excellence is a train trip. The first thing they have to do is unpack the old cultural baggage they're carrying around—this involves exploring where they came from, what was good about it and what wasn't. Dealing with the old baggage and discarding what we don't need creates room for the new.

Then everyone boards the train and the journey begins. Each stop along the way is an outpost of our corporate culture—teamwork, sense of urgency, delighting customers, and continuous improvement. They get off and involve themselves in a classroom experience. Then they fill out postcards about what they've learned and send them "home"—these actually end up on the classroom bulletin board.

As the journey progresses, they get involved in a simulation: Something is killing quality. They have to work in teams to solve the puzzle of what that is. At each stop there's a game, and if their table wins they get another clue. We do a lot of reward and recognition at AT&T Universal Card Services, so there's a lot of that in the program, too.

At the end of the journey they talk about the souvenirs they picked up along the way. We go back to the packing and unpacking exercise, and people talk about what they discovered and how it compared to what they hoped for and expected. They find they have experienced the key elements of our culture, what we believe in, what the environment is like—and have interacted with each other within that new framework.

Teaching should happen regularly, as part of a person's work. It should be a chance for everyone, teachers and students alike, to renew their commitment to the company's cultural values, as well as a way of monitoring how well those values are working in practice.

Roger Easom, manager of management education, the Leadership Institute, Federal Express: Federal Express has a philosophy—People, Service, Profit—that is the cornerstone of our culture. When employees' formal complaints signaled a shift away from the *people* focus, senior and executive management took action to ensure managers are taught how to balance *service* and *profit* with *people*. We set up the Leadership Institute as a place where managers could be educated in ways to keep the FedEx vision as vital as it was the day the company was founded. We also developed the Federal Express Manager's Guide, a book of management principles which serves as a basic textbook for all FedEx leadership training.

Anne Swearingen Duty, manager, Employee Communications Area, Federal Express: The Institute offers courses in every aspect of management. In their first forty-five days on the job, all new managers have to complete Management Principles 1, which is a five-day basic leadership course. It sets the tone for managerial style and behavior. They learn how to conduct a performance review, how to deal with an angry employee, *people*-intensive kinds of things. They don't learn nuts-and-bolts things like doing your budget—they'll get that elsewhere.

Some other popular courses include Beyond Unions, Coaching for Commitment, and Interpersonal Dynamics, which helps managers see themselves as their employees may see them.

Roger Easom: The courses are taught by experienced senior managers and managing directors. They teach for two years and then rotate back into their regular jobs. The classes are student-driven; the facilitators, called preceptors, are there to guide what is usually a very lively discussion. The preceptors bring reality to the classroom; as successful managers themselves, they understand the pressures, shortcomings, and needs of their students.

You'd be amazed at the effect a month of classes can have on a stressed-out manager who—through no fault of his own—has lost sight of FedEx's original vision. It's a chance to put all those day-to-day anxieties on the shelf, take a deep breath, and go back to the basics that made this company work in the first place.

Along with the Institute's regular classroom courses, we have a televised course on our closed-circuit channel, FXTV. The course strives to stay topical, focusing on changes—external and internal—that affect us. One segment will deal with new legislation from Washington, for example, the next with new company policy concerning smoking in the workplace.

At the end of each broadcast, managers sign on to a computer system called Quest and take a multiple-choice test. If they pass, they get three hours of credit applied to their forty-hour annual training requirement. If they flunk, they can watch the program again and take the test again.

Sometimes informal teaching, done on an ad hoc *basis, can be the best way to keep the weeds from growing.*

Jim Abolt, vice president, Organization and Management Development, Frito-Lay: I was working with our operations folks to help them focus more on satisfying their downstream customers. They were having a hard time grasping how important customer service is.

I'll never forget the day I brought a salesman named Carl in to talk with some of the operations folks. He explained to them in language they understood the importance of customer satisfaction. "Let's take a look at how you guys in operations treat us salespeople," he said. "You take our order and tell us not to worry. Then the order comes in short. We don't know why. You have a bunch of excuses—then you tell us it's okay we didn't get it.

"What if we went into a Kroger's supermarket and told them, 'Hey, I don't know when you're going to get your product, probably sometime Tuesday or Wednesday, but listen, when you do get it, even if it's not exactly what you ordered, don't worry about it, you'll still be satisfied.' You people are making us look bad and we don't like it."

Carl had everybody in the room laughing, but the message he was delivering came through loud and clear: If they didn't focus on satisfying the customer, he wouldn't be able to satisfy the customer either, and everything would fall apart.

The single most important lesson that must be taught is the permanence of change.

Jim Abolt: We are now undergoing a third wave of cultural change designed to make our reengineered environment self-sustaining. We reserve the right to get smarter at what we do.

We drive home to our plant managers how serious we are about reengineering, how it isn't some passing fad. There's still a lingering attitude of: This will blow over. Well, the fact is, it won't. We are firmly committed to the principles and processes of reengineering as an ongoing, ever-evolving way to ensure that this company just keeps getting better and better.

We bring our managers down to headquarters for a week-long education session. We let them know what the future looks like and why it's in their best interest to get with the program. We build their leadership skills. We align everyone's thinking.

Dave Zemelman, senior vice president of Human Resources, Frito-Lay: The first thing we did with our senior executives was to describe our company values and then have everyone work together in creating a document that spelled them out. We searched our archives and found the founders' original statement of company values. They are very close to the ones we want to guide us into the future. We took those original principles and updated them with the more contemporary values we are striving to instill. One builds on the other. Just participating in writing that document forced people to think about what Frito-Lay stands for.

Working on this document was thought provoking and provided an opportunity to stand back and take the long view of what we're doing, what we're about, and where we're going.

The next step was peer feedback, which is nothing more than filling out confidential surveys on each other. How do you work? Are you perceived as part of the team? That feedback is compiled and then shared with you privately. It is also read by the president of the company, who then has a one-on-one with each manager.

After a manager has had a chance to digest his feedback, he gets up in front of the group and shares what he has learned—what he does well, areas where he needs to change—and then leads a discussion about himself. It's a little like Alcoholics Anonymous; a free-form exchange that covers strengths, weaknesses, and an appeal for help. It works. Most of the managers come away feeling much better than when they went in. They think it's going to be like root canal. In general, people are more reinforcing of positives than critical of negatives. But it's important to bring up the negative stuff and take a good, hard look at it. This process started to change the way we worked together as a senior team.

We replicate this phenomenon with our field managers in our leadership forums. These sessions demonstrate that there's nowhere to hide. Change is here and it's not going away. It's not a matter of flattening the organization and then going back to the same hierarchical relationships but with less folks in the middle. It's about an ongoing, never-ending commitment to doing things better. The message is: Learn to live with it, learn to thrive in it. We've taken the first steps and we are not turning back.

DOING

Behavioral change can be accelerated if you can formalize the "doing" beyond managers, creating what Arizona Public Service describes as "champions of change" and "cultural warriors."

Armando Flores, vice president of Human Resources, Arizona Public Service: Champions of cultural change are employees who display team-spirited behavior and are prime candidates for influencing others. They take part in a weeklong session that reviews the objectives of the company in terms of strategy, mission, and culture.

Then they are asked to go out and champion cultural change in their respective areas: to influence others through staff meetings, one-on-one communication, and positive confrontations. We have these "cultural disciples" all around the company; it's more effective than having a cultural change staff that goes in, explains what we want, and then moves on.

We have these cultural warriors at every level of the company, from truck drivers to computer programmers to senior managers. The idea is that they continuously model the culture that we're striving for, and are also available, on a day-to-day basis, to help educate and influence their peers. In addition, many of them take a certain amount of time every month to go around to other parts of the company and talk about APS culture and the need for every employee to champion our new culture.

A good culture is maintained by designing a way for people to monitor their own behavior. Everyone must know how they are doing if we are to expect them to assume accountability.

Richard Fowler, assistant vice president, Great Lakes region, USAA: In addition to better-designed customer surveys and the use of focus groups, we've added the capability to get immediate feedback after a customer phone call. The idea of recovery from mistakes was much on our minds. We had studied other companies and learned that they only heard about customer dissatisfaction approximately 10 percent of the time, when a customer called or wrote. There was also the positive side to take into account, too—we knew that most of our representatives delivered excellent service, although there was no record of it.

At the end of a customer call, the rep will say: "If you are willing to stay on the phone for ten or fifteen seconds after I hang up, you could give us some valuable feedback." After the rep hangs up, a voice response system says: "If the service you just received exceeded your expectations, press one. If it met your expectations, press two. If it was deficient, press three. If you would like to leave any message for management's attention, you may do so at the tone. You can say anything you want."

The beauty of this is that it's primarily monitored in the units, so they own the response system. On the other hand, the possible weakness is that the rep has control over whose comments get recorded. We have to make them want the response that may be critical as well as the one that's sure to be complimentary. We have to make it totally non-threatening. We aren't going to use this to beat up on people.

It's the nature of our business sometimes to have to deliver bad news. The customer may say: "What? You won't insure me just because I've had seventeen auto accidents?" That kind of hostility could cause a good rep to get bad grades. The way to deal with this is to keep the information within the unit, where people quickly identify the cranks and discount their comments.

The reps get scores at the end of each day. One of our reps, after hearing a lot of glowing opinions about herself, said to me: "I used to think of this job as a production line and that every call would be just as boring and routine as the last one. Now that I know I'm being graded, it matters to me more. I like to know how good a job I did."

The reps and their team leaders listen to the comments, which often go beyond the service at hand to broader company issues. They then respond immediately. The member could get a letter, signed by the unit manager, in two or three days. It might say: "We understand that you were concerned about our insurance rates and here is what we are doing about it." It shows the customer that we do listen.

Over time, certain reps tend to do exceptionally well and others don't. Patterns emerge. We study these patterns and use the knowledge we gain to improve our training, stressing the qualities of the reps who consistently get positive responses.

Designing accountability systems can also be a powerful way to tell a customer that your company considers their business important.

Rick Zaffarano, director of warehouse operations, Hannaford Brothers: We use customer surveys and have customer-satisfaction teams. Every load that leaves the warehouse has a survey form that we ask the driver and the receiver at the store to fill out. In the case of an error, we require a personal contact, so the loader who made the mistake will call the store and talk to the person who filled out the form to explain what happened and apologize. Our customer-satisfaction teams have established contacts in all the stores. They check in with them on a regular basis.

LIVING

Living a culture demands that everyone deal with potential problems proactively.

Armando Flores: We have what we call the "gap attack." We analyze where we want to be, and then we find the areas where there's a critical gap between that goal and where we are at present. Then we do gap attacks. The gap attack starts by putting together a game plan on how to close the gap, and then assigning a team of people to carry out the plan.

As everyone lives the culture, the change will become pervasive, energizing veterans and transforming new hires.

Mike Parrish, vice president and general manager, Nucor: Our steel mill in Jewett, Texas, is pretty typical of the company as a whole. Although steel is a very labor-intensive business, we run very lean. There are about 450 men working at this plant. Front-line supervision is on the mill floor, where we have a rolling-mill manager and a casting manager. Then we have a controller, a sales manager, and a maintenance manager. That's a total of five managers. They all report directly to me, and I report directly to the company president. Those five men are given a lot of freedom to run their departments; there's nobody looking over their shoulder. And the same is true for the company as a whole. Each plant has a lot of autonomy; we make our own decisions with very little involvement from headquarters.

As we've grown over the years, we've sometimes hired people from Bethlehem, US Steel, and other companies. They're used to a very formal agenda, a lot of memos and rigid lines of communication. We don't operate that way. You'll find a lot of face-to-face communication around here, managing by walking the floor. It's very informal. Sure, we sometimes write memos, but they're usually handwritten and delivered in person.

I don't have a personal secretary. It's not a matter of policy, it's just my choice. I have a computer and printer, and type most of my own letters. If I need help in coordinating travel, I can call the personnel department, but often as not I'll just arrange my own flight. Most other managers do the same. If they do have a secretary, it's usually someone with double duties—half-time secretarial, half-time billing and collections. The people who come to us from other companies quickly get Nucorized—we get that big company mentality out of their system and replace it with our no-fat way of thinking.

Sometimes merely changing your physical space can help reinforce a cultural change.

Richard Fowler: A lot of reengineering has to do with the more logical use of physical space. Managers now have more detailed knowledge of, and more contact with, other corporate functions, simply because they are working side by side. The claims manager sits near an underwriter. They talk, get to know each other, develop a rapport. Instead of having to make a formal request for an underwriting consultation on a difficult claim case, and sending that request by interoffice mail or E-mail, the manager simply turns around in his chair and gets an answer.

It's not enough to tell people a new culture is good for the customer; to get employees to participate completely, they have to see how the new values are good for them, too.

Jim Abolt: I remember going to a plant and asking folks if they preferred their work life or their personal life. They all told me they liked their personal life a lot better. I then asked where they had more responsibility, and they answered in their personal life. They would mention car payments, raising kids, paying for food. They said at work all they had to do was show up and do what they were told. I told them we wanted to increase their responsibility level at work.

A lot of people resisted at first. I asked them if they'd like it if the company took over their car and house payments and took care of their kids. People said that would be great. Then I told them, we would also get to decide what kind of car they drive, what color they paint their house, where their kids go to school. "Whoa, no way," was the response.

That's when I told them that we're trying to create a work environment similar to the one they have at home. You are going to be responsible for cost results just like you are responsible for paying for your car. Since you are responsible for paying for your car, you can pick any car you want. If you are responsible for costs, you can now make decisions about costs. We try to get the point across that responsibility isn't something that is daunting. Responsibility means freedom, too, and people find that liberating.

AND NOW THE DON'TS

There are some people who argue that cultural change is impossible, that values and behaviors are too deeply rooted in people to expect them to change. But the prior examples prove that behavior is indeed changing in our companies. Accomplishing this change is a necessary part of reengineering work. But in your eagerness to get on with living the question of culture, you can't ignore these five don'ts:

1. Don't live too long with people who refuse to change their behavior, especially if their work is important to achieving your reengineering goals. Your tolerance of old behaviors signals that you are not serious about change.

2. The above applies to all people, managers as well as workers. This is a new democracy!

3. Don't expect people to change how they behave unless you change what they do; that is, their work must be designed to allow them to act differently.

4. Don't expect cultural change to happen immediately. Although you may achieve some early results, a complete cultural change is usually measured in terms of years (hopefully just a few) rather than months.

5. Don't articulate a new or updated set of values and then delay reengineering your management processes to support them. More on this in the next chapter.

CHAPTER 8

HOW WILL *WE* DO OUR WORK?

*The reason managers can actually manage in today's
markets—running the race that begins at top speed, then
gradually pick up the pace—is that they are not alone.
They are "we."
"We" with our subordinates (if that's the right word); "we"
with our bosses (if that's the right word); and "we" with our
peers (which is surely the right word).
In some organizations today, the right word is associates,
which may well be the best word of all.*

Association, collaboration, cooperation—all these relationships, in their own way, form an underlying precept of this book. Understanding them and acting on them always pays off—in inspiration, support, and morale, the ultimate moral conditions of success.

Pragmatically, however, collaboration is simply what we need to get our work done. It extends (or should extend) well beyond our immediate associates—to our customers, suppliers, vendor partners (to whom we may outsource parts of our operations), and occasionally even to our competitors, as when the joint pursuit of an opportunity seems likely to assure mutual success.

But let's get specific here. . . .

WHAT SORT OF WORK ARE WE TALKING ABOUT?

Every business has core processes: new product development, customer service, order fulfillment, and the like. In *Reengineering the Corporation*, we showed how focusing on the fundamental redesign of these core operational processes offered a company the best leverage for raising performance.

A single task such as answering the phone, sending a service vehicle to a neighborhood after a power outage, or filling out an order form does not of itself create value. What creates value is the particular "assembly" of such tasks: the way each one relates to another, the way authority and accountability are distributed, and the way process performance is measured and judged. To do this properly is to do it radically, subjecting each task to fearless questioning. *What is it for?*—that's the question underlying all other questions. What purpose is advanced by this task? How does it relate to what the customer wants, deserves, needs, or could be induced to need? How does it relate to the overall goals of the business?

Not all operational processes will survive this sort of questioning; some are closer to the core of the business than others. New product development is at the core of a pharmaceutical business; customer service is at the core of a bank. If you can identify those key operational processes, reassemble the work that goes into them in line with the core mission of the business (always keeping in mind that further changes will be required), the impact on the bottom line will be quick and dramatic.

This was the promise of reengineering, and for hundreds of companies over the last two years, the promise has been kept. Other companies have not seen these big results, often because they haven't yet focused on the *core* operational processes. Some hesitated, choosing instead to test reengineering by starting with non-critical processes—the mail room, say. Others, even more cautious or self-defeating, decided to reengineer mail distribution precisely to avoid reengineering the core.

In the end, though, some sort of change is inevitable. Our competitors, our customers, and our new technological tools, all combine to force us to operate at whole new levels of efficiency. But to reach these new levels we must constantly ask ourselves the *work questions*: What work must we do? How can we do it better—much better?

Reaching these new levels also demands that we constantly ask ourselves the *management questions*. What work should we managers do? What value do we add to the enterprise? What are our processes good for, and how do they serve the goals of the company? These questions would be tough to take in any context; nobody likes to have to defend his or her role or worth. But in the context of reengineering they're particularly challenging, because answering them effectively demands that we redistribute authority and accountability in work processes. It's crucial that we move much of management's command-and-control function to the front lines when we redesign and reassemble tasks. So sooner or later we must give management processes the same hard scrutiny that we gave work processes. The question has to be faced: What is there left for managers to do?

The answer, you'll be relieved to hear, is that there's a great deal for us to do—all of it absolutely necessary to the success of an enterprise. The past few years have taught me that during a period of high change there are five core management processes: *mobilizing*, *enabling*, *defining*, *measuring*, and *communicating*. (Please note that among the traditional management functions, only those *dys*functions—commanding and controlling—have gone by the board.) Let's take these management processes one at a time, and see how they must change.

MOBILIZING

Mobilization is the process by which a company and its people are at least brought to the point where they accept the changes that reengineering entails—and at best to where they are ready and willing to make them happen. In Chapter 4 I explored what managers must put into such an effort: essentially, a candid, company-wide campaign of persuasion by *reasons*, and a compelling picture of the future. Why? Because for people to change both what they do and how they behave (and potentially what they value), they must have an honest and detailed description of the case for change and a vision of the future that is better than the present.

One question about mobilization may still remain unclear, however: the question of downsizing. Too often, unfortunately, the only goal of mobilization turns out to be *cost reduction*.

It's not that cost reduction isn't a good idea for many companies. Some still carry heavy loads of bureaucracy from the era of Smooth Sailing; others packed on all sorts of extraneous functions in the go-go 1980s. Cost reduction is an imperative if these companies want to stay competitive, or in business at all.

For an enterprise manager, unfortunately, saying "Let's mobilize for cost reduction!" is a little like saying, "Anyone up for the funeral?" You may find some takers, but they won't be in the best of spirits. I think, for example, of the manager who told me recently, "We don't really know how to do reengineering in our company; so what we do is, we regularly downsize the company and leave it to the three people who are left to figure out how to do their work differently." They will probably figure it out—and be miserable in the process. They will *certainly* figure out that this is a helluva way to do reengineering.

In fact, downsizing and reengineering are two different things, although we frequently see them together. But to see downsizing without reengineering, as the manager I just mentioned surely discovered, is tragic. For one thing, reengineering is the way to redesign work for those people remaining in the company. It may be the only way for a company to fix its systemic operating problems. And it is certainly a way to build operational excellence.

Just downsizing is almost all downside; even the promised cost reduction often turns out to be an illusion. Alone downsizing just reduces capacity *and* capability. And costs just get added back if business improves. Reengineering may be painful, disruptive, and threatening, too, but it can also be thrilling and challenging, when the new operating vision contains objectives of significant growth, better products, and better service. And it's precisely because the prospect of it arouses these positive feelings that reengineering is the perfect endeavor—second only to a start-up—around which to mobilize. (In some cases, it is like a start-up: redesigning the work with a blank sheet of paper.)

In fact, I'd like to push the argument further. The essence of Emersonian thinking, for managers, is to keep alive in every enterprise—big and small, old and not so old—the spirit of the start-up. This is not easy. In a start-up, every course is by necessity experimental, a zig and a zag; in a start-up, everyone knows—*everyone*—that everything they do counts (and that the status game counts for very little); because in a start-up, of course, there is no corpse of memory, no history, that must constantly and painfully be judged.

These conditions are not available in older, larger companies—not until disaster looms, if then. But that's the challenge of mobilization for today's manager, perhaps the key challenge of our work. It is to convince everyone in the organization that "new days" are no longer determined by the inexorable movement of the calendar, but changing markets, changing technologies, changing competitors, and demanding customers.

ENABLING

It's not enough to get your people mobilized, energized, ready and willing every day for a "new day's" struggle. You've got to give them the wherewithal. That requires enabling; redesigning work so that people can exercise their skills and capabilities to the fullest extent possible—then stepping back and letting it happen. The more fashionable term here, of course, has been *empowering*. I've said it myself: Reengineering demands that managers empower people to do the new operational work and to do whatever it takes to serve the customer's needs.

That's all very true. The trouble with *empowerment* is that the word has been repeated so often, and so mindlessly, that it has lost its power. When reengineering first talked about the concept, many managers behaved as if empowering others meant disempowering themselves. They really didn't give an inch, keeping the power to make decisions to themselves, but they often talked *"empowerment"* fluently, until the word became so puffed up with hot air that it died and went to heaven with all the other fine old phrases that no longer have any meaning.

Furthermore, reengineers insist, a shift in *power* isn't what we need today; it doesn't help us find or satisfy customers. For that, we need a shift in authority and accountability. Reengineering recognizes a key distinction between two kinds of authority. *Ex officio* authority is your title and place on the organizational chart; it says nothing about your personal skills and leadership ability. Existential authority, on the other hand, grows out of how you actually practice your particular skills and leadership ability in a particular operational (or management) process. In Mr. Sloan's sort of corporation, without *ex officio* authority you couldn't have existential authority. In the reengineered corporation, it has to be reversed. Reengineering managers are always looking for ways to foster existential authority, often by bypassing the *ex officio* kind, or by getting rid of it altogether.

To accomplish this shift, however, managers do have to give up something. Not power (whatever that means), but something quite precise—*control*, or as we've been saying, command-and-control. And that should kick up some fear. The feeling of being in control is the closest many managers ever come to the true personal satisfactions of existential authority; for many others, it's the only thing that stands between them and panic.

Managers on the edge of panic, of course, will not survive the revolution, but those who choose to work the change may well discover the nice paradox of control: Giving it up is the best way to get it. Managers who cling to feelings of being in control are like sailors who try to steer by diving overboard to push the rudder around. This makes sense if the thing is stuck, or if you want to learn how it works. Otherwise, it's best to direct the boat with a light hand on the wheel.

Rick Zaffarano of Hannaford Brothers has discovered firsthand how hard it is to give up control. "My own thinking tends to be hierarchical in certain situations," he told us. "Sometimes giving orders seems to be the natural way to handle a problem," he confessed. "I like to be able to say yes or no without having to confer all the time and seek consensus. So there are some drawbacks for me in the new order, but I realize it's the right thing to do."

Zaffarano's "right thing" would look drastic to a traditional manager. His title is director of Warehouse Operations, but he is actively working to eliminate the job. (Not himself from the company: He told us that after he cut his current position from the budget, he'd like to "slip into a corporate resource role, or a mentor's role.") "My goal is to create a DCLT [distribution center leadership team] strong enough to manage the whole distribution center without a director," Zaffarano explained.

He was doing this by redistributing working authority in the warehouse among seven teams (of 20 workers each) and two mentors (people who act as coaches in one of several broad areas: equipment, cultural development, team development, return on investment, productivity, and efficiency). Each team has an informal leader, called an operations coordinator, who meets with the others in a DCLT. Mentor expertise is called on as the occasion demands.

If *enabling*, in the end, came easier to Zaffarano than it does for some others, part of the credit must go to headquarters, which trusted him enough to let him trust others. "My boss used to work here, so he has a pretty good sense of what we're doing," he said. "But I haven't talked to anyone at corporate about the whole DCLT idea. I've been given a lot of autonomy. I like taking the risk that's involved, because risk-taking creates peak performance. It's my idea and I think it's great, and I have the support I need. I'm going to play it out, and we'll see what happens."

The "it" he's going to play out will seem pretty radical to some managers:

We're creating a process that allows hourly and salaried associates to make all the decisions. Suppose, for example, a proposal for a change in benefits, let's say an extra week of vacation, came from one of the seven teams. The DCLT and the team's representatives would discuss it, and the DCLT would either agree, or disagree, or suggest some changes. Let's say further that they agreed, and that all the seven teams, after having it run by them by their representative, also agreed. In that event, the DCLT would say, "Okay, we'll make the recommendation to corporate for you, or you can come with us and we'll make it together." Of course the DCLT would disapprove of anything that seemed to violate a business imperative, as would the people at headquarters; and a mentor might vote against a proposal, too, if it ran against the interests he represented. But if the proposal got past these obstacles, we'd put it into effect.

Five years ago, Zaffarano's scheme would have been called "worker democracy." Three years ago, it would have been called "empowerment." But whatever his DCLT is called, it works—and it works because he has built into his redistributed authority structure a hard-line concern (a "culture," we might say) for the *quality* of the teams' *work*. There is very little chance that self-management at the shop-floor level will distract from what the self-managers are there for.

Zaffarano's reengineered authority structure has its own internal monitors, he explained:

In addition to picking a team coordinator, the team picks a "Star Point," who is the coordinator on a specific [work] function. For example, the operations Star Points make sure the teams have schedules, the safety Star Points discuss ways to improve the physical environment, and so on. We also rotate these positions, the reasoning being that we can bring people into contact with fresh ideas, and foster appreciation of what it takes to manage.

The system has some problems—teams and therefore Star Points are on different schedules, and people get good at managing/coordinating some function, then are rotated out and leave a void that's hard to fill. Then there are people who want to leave because they need a break from the pressure. We don't pay any extra for it: We didn't want people to do it for the money. On the whole, though, the system has been working real well.

As Rick Zaffarano can testify, enabling is a very tricky affair. Some cultures will actively or passively repel every attempt to disseminate authority and accountability throughout a work process. Many individuals will do the same, often without being aware of it themselves. "Leave it to management" is the most common way people refuse to accept responsibility at work and refuse to make any emotional investment in their job. At first, the tactic looks like a good bet, protecting people against blame, failure, and regret. In the end, though, it does the opposite. By breeding apathy and boredom, it virtually guarantees blame, failure, and regret.

The good news is that no genius is required to figure this out. Even the worst of the old-style authoritarian cultures (which often pretend to be anti-authoritarian cultures) is open to change; people are hungry for it. Still, just as enterprise managers must prepare their associates for the ordeal of reengineering, managers at all levels must carefully test the culture they're working in for its ability to take broadly disseminated authority and accountability. Some cultures will take it better than others: They will require relatively little cultivation. Others will require harrowing, plowing, fertilizing, and endlessly alert weeding.

Then managers must "let go." We heard in an earlier chapter how Rick Zaffarano, faced with a delivery crisis caused by a blizzard, overcame his fears and let his people decide how to solve the problem. We didn't hear him draw the moral. It is, once again, the need for trust.

> I think the reason most managers won't buy into the sort of thing we are doing here is because they can't make that leap of faith. Relying on past experiences, they assume the worst: People will take advantage of every situation, they can't control their schedules, they're selfish. That's how we are brought up to supervise and why we feel compelled to control. Well, running this warehouse has really increased my trust in people.

The only way that trust can be maintained over time is to have a culture that purposefully assures that people will behave the way the business needs them to behave.

DEFINING

Defining a company's ambition is a process that has been on the managerial agenda ever since there's been a profession of management. Think of "management by objectives." But the process has taken on new scope and urgency in the present historical context.

Remember, first, that the promise of reengineering is more than just survival in revolutionary times. The promise is that you will take on the spirit of revolution, internalize it, and *thrive*! And how do you fulfill that promise? The answer is simple, but not easy—by dedicating your leadership to continuous experimentation, wily zigging and zagging.

Managing by experimentation demands courage and great care. Your questioning has to be constant, an unflinching comparison between what you wanted and what you got. You must learn from the comparisons, and then learn to act on what you've learned. Unless you can subject your decision-making to a ruthless and continuous *judgment by results*, all your zigs and zags will only be random lunges in the dark, sooner or later bound to land you on the rocks.

The first step in the process, defining the objectives you want, sounds easy enough. You simply examine the "realities" of the situation—the upside and downside risks of the opportunity (to sell a new product, say) against the assets in money, time, and talent that you must throw behind the decision to exploit the opportunity—and then make a sound judgment call based on a "reasonable" set of objectives.

Sorry, but it's not that obvious, not to a reengineer anyway. When I hear managers setting "reasonable" and "realistic" objectives for a work process, or for their team, division, or company, I begin to wonder whether I've made myself clear. Reengineers think in terms of *radical* or (if "radical" is too politically charged for your company) *very ambitious* objectives. We think that way for good reasons. What companies actually require to thrive in today's revolutionary climate is seldom anything so "reasonable" and "realistic" as a 10 percent improvement in some performance measure or other. What we actually require is more often something like a 50 percent improvement, or a 75 percent improvement.

Moreover, even where a 25 percent improvement—in order fulfillment, for example—might do instantaneous wonders for the bottom line, it's doubtful whether it will do any wonders for the competitive strength of the organization over the long haul. That's because minor objectives require only minor changes in work and managerial processes, whereas long-term competitive strength usually requires major (and continuous) changes.

Defining objectives is a tool of management, as everyone knows. But reengineers know that defining objectives can also be a powerful way to change institutions—or institutionalized ways of doing things. To do that, we have to set goals that repeatedly force us "back to square one," back to the "clean slate." That's where the most frightening and fundamental questions arise: not just the usual questions about how we can do this operation better, but whether we should be doing it at all. It's only through this kind of radical critique that we can hope to get rid of all the fragmentation, complexity, and bureaucracy within our work and management processes. And often the best way to get started on that critique is to define our goals radically—not 25 percent "better," but "100 percent."

Perhaps the best example of modest goal definition we see these days is downsizing and outplacing. Lowering headcounts and getting rid of allegedly superfluous functions, for all the pain they cause, is *intellectually* pretty easy. You may think long and hard about the pros and cons of doing it, but once you've done it you can stop thinking. You don't have to worry about the operations you've got left. The removal of the deadwood should let the green wood flourish, right?

Well, no. To gain and sustain real competitive advantages, cost reduction may be necessary, but it is never sufficient. It may even be destructive, establishing a new set of illusions to take the place of the old set. Instead, you must define real, positive objectives, not negative and possibly illusory ones. Set yourself truly ambitious goals for reducing your delivery cycles, your product development and production times; radically increase the quality and timeliness of your installation and repair services; get absolutely ruthless about the deployment of capital. Define your goals in this way, and the whole company will transform itself in the wake of them.

Finally, radical change through radical goal definition holds out a secret satisfaction to the manager who pulls it off. If you can learn to do what other managers in your industry thought to be impossible, you will not only thrive, you will literally redefine the industry.

MEASURING

Reengineering's great contribution to the management process of measurement has been to help keep the accountancy focused on what really matters for the business. It is ultimately in terms of results for customers—their pleasure and/or pain—that we can measure a company's performances, whether people's, products', or processes'.

Traditionally, most of our business measurement processes have been financially based—produced by accountants, designed for accountants (or regulators), not by or for managers. Measures come in the form of balance sheets, monthly profit and loss statements, and ROIs. They are often damage reports, telling us that we performed poorly only after the fact. They tell us nothing about what we do today or tomorrow. We can extrapolate from them, but we know how dangerous that is. Nor do most of our measurement processes tell us about those other objectives that a reengineer wants to constantly scrutinize, such as cycle time and quality, or if they do, reports come too late for us to take action. On the whole, today's measurement processes don't really help us manage.

And worse, our desks are cluttered with reports, many of which we seldom look at. I recall a particular meeting not long ago with the senior management of a large corporation. Everyone was present except the CEO, who we were informed would arrive late. As the meeting began, the CFO was complaining that he was having trouble producing a report that the CEO required ten days after the close of each quarter. The data was hard to collect, and he had to maintain a room full of clerks to get it on the CEO's desk on time. Not even computer power could help. At that moment, the CEO entered the room, and I asked the CFO to repeat his story. He did so with passion and frustration, and the CEO replied, "What report is that?"

We all have reports that seem to flow constantly, and it is almost a law of thermodynamics that we aren't able to shut them off. But now, as we rethink our purpose, define new ambitions, and look to radically improve our key business metrics, we must identify the process results we want to measure that will accurately predict our business performance. And we must focus the whole organization on these key process results.

The failure of the "machine" model of the corporation is partially a failure of measurement focus. Inevitably, in even the best of such companies, performances are never really judged by standards of utility to the customer. Instead, they're judged by how well they work for the supposed bosses of the hierarchy, from the CEO down to the shop foreman, the team supervisor, the union's business agent (if any), or the worker himself. In other words, performance measurement is entirely a function of internal requirements, either bureaucratic, "political," or personal. Dave Sanders, director of Business Process Reengineering at Detroit Edison, recounted a classic case in point at his own company:

In the past, when schedules were missed, the company's internal measures provided a lot of hiding space. For example, when a storm knocked out power, we were supposed to send someone within thirty minutes. To meet that goal, a dispatcher might send someone who couldn't do the work. Perhaps it was too complex, perhaps the dispatcher knew this. Too bad, the dispatcher sent the person anyway: The important thing (for him) was to meet the thirty-minute deadline. Now this is ridiculous, a perfect example of internally focused measurement. The last thing the customer wants is a guy sitting in a truck who can't do the work.

Today, nobody gets any points for sending out someone who can't do the work. That measure was thrown out and replaced with one that measures how quickly we satisfy the customer.

The difficulty with management's traditional measuring practices is precisely there: It has an apparently undefeatable tendency to focus inward toward the men and women at the buttons and levers, rather than outward toward the customer, where it belongs. That tendency is hardly surprising: Measurement means evaluation; judgments must be made. But, none of us likes to be judged; many don't even like to judge. Hence the salient place of judging and being judged among the ten items in our Culture of Willingness. But hence, too, the inevitable inward bent of a corporation's standards of measurement: People want to shield themselves from judgment, deflect it, share it as widely as possible, muddle it with bureaucratic process, anything to avoid standing in the glare of a clear, unequivocal measure of their worth.

That's why, in the end, we have to acknowledge the usefulness of the new trends in personal performance measurement—peer evaluation and the assessment of managers by their direct reports, as difficult as they may be to execute. It used to be, in the old regime of the "machine" company, that nothing was measured that couldn't be translated straight into numbers—outputs, bottom lines, etc. Today an attempt is made to measure all sorts of things—"leadership," "cooperation," "decisiveness," and the like—that are hard to quantify. They can only be judged subjectively, by the people they impact, measured in surveys, opinion polls, and so forth. This is what FedEx does with its Survey Feedback Action, a poll of employees' judgments of their managers and associates, as Anne Swearingen Duty explained:

Once a year, employees participate anonymously in SFA as they key their assessments of their immediate managers, upper management, and FedEx in general into the computer system. There are 32 statements on the SFA, including: "my manager helps us do our job better"; "my manager asks for my ideas about work"; "upper management tells us about company goals"; "people cooperate within my work group." There are four reported possible scores—favorable, favorable/unfavorable, unfavorable, and no answer.

When we managers get the results, we go into our offices, close our doors, pore over the numbers, and wonder what we might do differently. Then we go to the second step, which is the feedback session where the managers meet with their employees to get at the root causes of the problems the SFA has revealed.

The third step is action. Every manager has to develop his own action plan, matching root causes with specific corrective action and detailing how and when this action will be taken.

Many managers will say that SFA carries reengineering a bit too far. College professors may now routinely submit to this kind of "consumer report" from their students. But students *do* consume teaching; they *are* in some sense the professor's customers. Likewise, managers must recognize that employees will have some of the characteristics of customers; if our people don't enthusiastically buy into our reengineering plans, we will inevitably fail. The danger, however, is that this kind of measuring can easily lead to abuse, specifically to one or another of the self- or inner bureaucratic obsessions that reengineering is supposed to root out.

Roger Easom has seen that pattern at FedEx's Leadership Institute, he admitted, and he has also seen the remedy:

> Sometimes SFA is used by an unscrupulous manager to hammer a lower-level manager. Sometimes there will be a work group reporting the same problems year after year. In cases like these, upper management has to take a very serious look at the underlying situation. In the latter case, for example, it could be an incompatible manager, but it could also be that some systemic problems were never addressed or corrected.
>
> SFA often has to be viewed with a sophisticated eye. But the superior manager—the kind we try to form at our Leadership Institute—anticipates problems. She invites continuous feedback. She keeps her finger on the pulse and doesn't have to wait for a once-a-year report card to know when something is veering off.

At AT&T Universal Card Services, as we've seen, the entire company is evaluated daily on over 100 different "indicators," as they're called. These range from questions such as whether there's been any downtime on the computer to questions about the professionalism and courtesy of the customer-service people on the phone. The performance bar on each indicator is raised steadily over time, and everyone in management, says Jim Kutsch, "spends a certain number of hours a month monitoring telephone associates, listening to them do their job. . . . It gives us a direct link and goes back to our determination to have continuous improvement in the quality of our service." Individual performance reviews are conducted by team leaders three times in the first year for people starting out, once a year after that. "However, there are feedback sessions every month," another manager assured us. "It's a continual process. Different managers have different ways of implementing it."

Finally, there's the most important measurement: the judgment by the customer. There are probably as many different ways of soliciting and reviewing customer evaluation of goods or services as there are companies trying to sell goods and services. The only important question, however, is a reengineer's question: How serious is the process? Does the "survey," or whatever, yield a candid, useful response from the customers? And, most vital, is anyone in the company really listening to it? In the reengineered company, the same testy questions must be applied to all measurements.

COMMUNICATING

About what? About the case for change. About the purpose around which we are mobilizing. About the culture and behavior we want and don't want. About the standards and objectives of our performances. About how we are doing against those standards and objectives. About why we are taking certain actions and how those actions serve our purpose.

You can't communicate with tired abstractions. People want to hear more than "we must act as a team." Eyes glaze over when managers spout generalities like "the customer is king." People want to know what these things mean for the company, for their work unit, and most of all, for them personally. So communicating is not just a job for the enterprise manager; it has to be the responsibility of all managers, as Dick Abdoo of Wisconsin Electric reminded me:

I regularly give the chairman's talk: why we need to change and where we are going. But I know that it's not enough. So we've produced videotapes that make the case, published newsletters, and used all types of media. But I know that's still not enough. What we need is the person who runs the cafeteria to understand what we're up to well enough so that he can communicate to everyone who works in that area why we are doing this, where we are going and what it means for all of us.

Articulating the goals and culture of the company is not, I'll bet, in the cafeteria manager's job description. That job, like many others, has just changed, radically. But Abdoo's objectives ask a lot of "communications." They require a full range of tools, not only different forms of media but also different words, stories, and pictures. Abstract ideas and objectives can often best be made real by telling stories. In fact, if the stories are powerful, they become part of the "lore" of the company that can shape culture and desired behaviors, as Bob O'Neal of AT&T Universal Card Services has discovered:

One of our corporate values is customer delight. Our competitors were basically satisfying their customers—the only way we were going to differentiate ourselves was to delight them. The telephone associates are empowered to make that happen.

We've got some stories that we tell in training, in Passport to Excellence, in meetings, to perpetuate the delight element of our culture. There's a famous one about the Alzheimer's patient. A card member called up to report his missing wife, an Alzheimer's patient who had wandered away and taken the AT&T Universal Card with her. He wanted to know if there had been any charge activity he could use to track her down. There hadn't been, but the associate took the man's information and over a period of several days tracked the account. Finally some food was charged on the card, we alerted the authorities, and they found the woman, who didn't know who or where she was. The family was reunited and the customer was delighted.

Just as there is something different in the character of how we do our "defining" in reengineering, there is something different in the character or quality of how we must communicate. I call it "authenticity," and wish I knew how to teach it.

Listen for it in the voices of people in this book. You are moved by it when you hear it. It goes beyond intelligence, good humor, sympathy, and understanding. These are necessary qualities for excellent communications, but they are not sufficient.

Authenticity has something to do with truth-telling and truth-facing, something to do with eloquence; but mostly, I'd guess, it has to do with the expression of a distinctive personality—who you are. The mystery lies in how and why some people are in touch with this distinctiveness of theirs and others are not. But there's no mystery, or not much, in the signs of it in people's speech. They make their speech their own by being concrete, specific, avoiding generalities, or, if they can't always do that, by giving them a spin all their own. I don't know whether God (or, as is sometimes said, the Devil) is in details, but authenticity certainly is.

It is authentic communication that brings people together into a community—listening, responding, confronting, asserting, and disputing—engaged in the perpetual process of change.

CHAPTER 9

CASES IN POINT—THINKING ABOUT MANAGEMENT PROCESSES

*Prescriptions for management processes, mine or anyone's,
are all well and good.
The important thing to remember is that, once in place,
they too must be judged by the light of a new day.*

Some things don't change, you may be happy to hear. Among them are the broad categories of specifically managerial work. Managers will continue, as they always have, enabling and communicating with workers, including managerial workers. They will also continue to define the work to be done and the standards it must meet, and to measure how well (or poorly) it meets those standards. Reengineering, however, calls into continual question all the traditional hows and wherefores of these processes. And this questioning, as I've discovered on my visits to the field, has unleashed a torrent of fresh thinking and acting on these topics.

ENABLING

Enabling and learning go hand in hand. Viewing mistakes as part of the learning process is crucial.

Leon Royer, executive director of Organizational Learning Services, 3M: This company has a long tradition of letting people make mistakes. It was part of Mr. McKnight's philosophy when he founded 3M in 1905. As long as someone is going in the right direction, a mistake is really about gaining knowledge. It's a learning experience.

As a leader, there's a strong temptation to step in and say, "Whoa, watch where you're going!" But then you've done the learning for your people. And once the mistake is made, you can never say, "If you had done it such and such a way, it would have worked." They know that.

Enabling means letting go of control. A symbolic action can be a potent means of signaling that you have indeed let go.

Leon Royer: In most corporations, signatures are a control tool. The frustrating question for employees becomes: How many signatures do I have to garner before I can go ahead and do something?

In my department, everyone signs for their own needs and expenditures. Some employees can approve larger expenditures than I can. That sends a powerful message, and we also remain within budget.

Enabling means that control must move all the way to the front line. A roadblock in the middle of the organization can stymie this movement and encourage old behaviors.

Tom Hardeman, senior ramp manager, FedEx, DFW Airport, Dallas: I force the reengineering issue by putting my managers in situations where they have to develop teams, delegate authority, and empower their employees. I pass a great deal of my own authority on to them with the understanding that they're going to follow suit with their own people. I meet one-on-one every week with each of my managers and we talk about how to develop a more effective management style. To put it very simply, there are two kinds of managers—the autocratic ones and the participative ones.

At my ramp facility, we do a tremendous volume of package sorting. Say we develop a missort problem. The autocratic manager is going to get faster results, probably by saying to his people: "You've got one week to fix this or I'm going to start firing some people." People get scared and the likelihood is the problem will get fixed, sooner rather than later.

The participative manager will say: "Let's meet as a group and put together a plan, using everyone's input." After that meeting, it'll probably take a couple of weeks before the problem is solved.

So what's the advantage of participation?

A month from now, the missort problem is going to reoccur for the autocratic manager because his employees used a quick fix to make him stop yelling. But the participative manager and his team will be humming along—because they took the time to fix the problem once and for all.

We've aspired to create "learning organizations" for years. The problem has been that the design of our work, and our management ideologies, have not allowed such organizations to develop. Reengineering wants them to flourish.

Jim Abolt, vice president of Organization and Management Development, Frito-Lay: I think it boils down to: Give me fish and I can eat for a day, teach me how to fish and I can eat forever. We have reengineering managers who go from plant to plant coaching people. It's very exciting for them to help the teams discover the answers for themselves, to watch them learn how to learn.

It all comes down to learning. If we could get an organization of 26,000 learners who are coming in every day and learning new ways to grow and improve, we would be the most competitive company in the world.

Requiring managers actually to do the work they'll be managing is the most powerful learning experience.

Kirby Dyess, vice president and director, Human Resources, Intel: Here at Intel we encourage managers to seek out hands-on, frontline experience. They find strengths that they never knew they had; they become better rounded. All of a sudden they have this exciting sense of "I can do this. I can coach others to do this." This helps them gain a perspective of *leadership* as opposed to *management*. They change their style because they have been there.

Enabling means tearing away the bureaucratic undergrowth that separates the worker's ability to help and the customer's desire to be helped.

Leon Royer: We minimize job descriptions and titles. Each person has his or her area of expertise, but we try to operate in a fluid manner; we want to bring the most knowledgeable person to bear in any given situation. If we have a customer problem in Taiwan, we may take a frontline plant-operation employee from here in St. Paul and fly her over there. Whoever is in the best position to delight the customer goes.

This is breaking some rules. Normally 3M doesn't fly non-exempt people around the world. Our answer is that we don't care about titles, we care about results.

Beware of the label "the person in charge." Is it someone who can actually help, or is it someone whose name happens to occupy the right box on the organization chart?

Richard Fowler, assistant vice president, Great Lakes region, USAA: Before reengineering, our claims units were made up of specialists. The focus of a unit stayed narrow—one took loss reports, another handled minor damage to autos, etc.

We thought this system resulted in customer calls being handled by a qualified specialist. But that wasn't the way customers saw it. All they knew was that their call got transferred around as their claim was processed, and they ended up talking to several people. For example, one person might take a loss report, another might work on the physical damage to the car, a third might get involved in the injury aspect. Then an appraiser assessed actual damages.

Today we have a system that isn't specialist-driven. Our front-line phone people are now generalists, trained in both policy service and claims, and can handle most common transactions themselves. They are supported by teams, enabling technology and specialist advisers. If they determine that it's a more serious accident, they'll transfer the call to a case manager with the appropriate skills. We take care of the irritating navigation through the bureaucracy. When a call comes in, the first requirement is to determine precisely where it needs to be sent so that it will never get handed off again. Customer satisfaction is up significantly.

People must know that their ideas will be listened to and, if they have merit, acted upon. If they do, it is possible to mobilize individual creativity on a very broad scale.

Gail Forsyth, manager "Your Ideas, Your Universe," AT&T Universal Card Services: "Your Ideas, Your Universe" produces nearly 3,000 suggestions annually from associates on how to improve performance in virtually every area of company operations. We receive ideas that directly improve the quality of service, and others that reduce costs or generate revenue. We give awards for these suggestions, ranging from silver dollars to gift certificates to substantial cash awards—up to $10,000—when the idea saves a lot of money. We also offer the option of making a donation to a designated charity.

One associate suggested that the company change its policy on overnight delivery of replacement cards by offering customers a choice of receiving the new card by 10 A.M. or 3 P.M. the following day. Previously we sent out all cards for the early delivery at considerably higher cost. The associate was awarded $6,000 for this suggestion.

Most associates average five or six suggestions a year; some submit an idea weekly. Overall, about two-thirds of the entire staff submits at least one idea per year. We publicize the program in various ways—on bulletin boards, through messages in the workstations, special promotions, and so on. People can submit ideas through a telephone hotline we've set up, in writing, or by fax.

We're committed to responding to each suggestion as quickly as possible; we acknowledge receipt and assign it to an evaluator (who is an appropriate expert in the subject) within twenty-four hours. The evaluators then have two weeks to respond. They look for any hidden problems that might impact a different department. We actually get very few bad ideas; only about 2 percent fail to get implemented.

I'm not convinced that the coach metaphor is always very useful, but here is a good description of enabling that uses the metaphor less misleadingly than usual.

Leon Royer: A leader has to let go. I call it liberation leadership. I like to use the metaphor of a hockey team. Who is the leader on a hockey team? It switches back and forth depending on who has the puck. And where is the ostensible leader, the coach? Sitting on the sideline without skates on. A coach can't tell his skaters where to take that puck. He can train them, psych them, prepare them. But when the buzzer sounds, it is the team that's out there on the ice, making individual decisions to achieve the goal.

My role as a coach is about three things. Number one is to give employees the tools they need to do their jobs. I'm not asking you to skate on tennis shoes, I give you skates. If you need a new computer system, my job is make sure you have it. Number two is to remove obstacles that hinder team performance. One common obstacle is bureaucracy; nothing clogs a team's arteries faster than bureaucracy. It is my responsibility to get those obstacles out of your way. Number three is to challenge the imagination. Imagination is where ideas and dreams come from. The trick is to excite that imagination by sharing information. How many fans or players would stick around to watch or play if they didn't know the score? Challenge the imagination by keeping the goals and expectations higher than your competition's.

The sum of all the coach's actions is to give the team ownership of the game and build trust. They know the coach isn't going to come out on the ice and tell them how to play the game. But they can report back to me and say, "I need a new stick," or "We have an interpersonal situation here that needs resolution."

The rules of the game are the values that you play by: ethical standards, quality, customer delight. When you win, there's a tremendous feeling of *shared* accomplishment. It's like winning the Stanley Cup; everyone wins equally.

Like all reengineered processes, enabling must be perpetually on-going to be successful, and it must touch everyone.

Dave Zemelman, senior vice president of Human Resources, Frito-Lay: We never give up. Change never stops. We don't want to reengineer just for the sake of reengineering. We do it to drive business results. We had a program called Managing the Journey. It was based on delivering consumer-winning quality in the marketplace, and on how we needed to change our processes and people to make that happen. It was a great success.

We followed that with an initiative called Continuing the Journey. In the first phase, the focus was on improving cost performance. Employees went through every plant from the bottom up and identified areas where money could be saved. This process had the added benefit of helping them understand the business. And the ideas they came up with ended up saving us $132 million.

Ron Rittenmeyer, vice president of Frito-Lay Business Systems: In the second phase of Continuing the Journey, we looked at every plant's performance in terms of quality, safety, cost, service, and turnover. We found the best one. The next step was to get every plant in the system up to that level. We brought together the top managers of all the plants to share strategy.

Every team at every plant had a volunteer who worked with management to determine how that unit could best reach its performance target. We gave the teams the authority to do what was needed. They could deal directly with their supplier, their receiver, the sales department, or even an outside supplier.

We wanted everyone working together. We wanted people to think not only about improving their function, but the functions on either side of them as well.

We set up guiding principles. For example, anything that adversely impacted quality or service—end of discussion. You couldn't cut back on maintenance; you could only improve up-time. The objective was not to take people out of the system. The objective was to take work out of the system.

We knew that at some point these changes would lead to downsizing. We agreed that we would handle those people with the appropriate dignity. We wouldn't shoot them in the back on Friday afternoon. It was each unit's job to come up with the most appropriate way to handle its own layoffs.

Lots of wonderful, innovative ideas came out of Continuing the Journey. For example, we started using steam energy that previously had been allowed to escape, and employees figured out how to make the packing machines work faster. Some of the changes seemed obvious in hindsight, but they're the kinds of things you overlook in the day-to-day stresses of running a business. When you step back and pull the whole process apart, suddenly they leap out at you. You smack your forehead and say: "I can't believe I didn't think of that."

Teams are also calling their counterparts in other plants and exchanging ideas and knowledge. The amount of cross-communication between our thirty-eight facilities is phenomenal. Employees who in the past operated within their narrow function are now calling other plants directly and talking to their peers, who they have never met, about common problems.

Continuing the journey is about continuing to change, about constantly staying open to new ideas, new processes, new ways to get better at what we do.

DEFINING

Customers aren't interested in your definition of a job well done. They just don't want any mistakes on their nickel. So set your objective at zero mistakes.

Dave Sanders, director of Business Process Reengineering, Detroit Edison: One of the areas we are working on is our response when the power goes out in a storm. The issue is time.

We're trying to greatly reduce how long it takes to restore power. Unfortunately, a lot of middle managers have lost sight of this as an overriding concern. Part of the problem is in their measures of success. They measure the number of customers who have lost power and the average time they've been without it. If I am one of those customers that didn't get restored, I could care less about those measurements.

So we're trying to drive home the need to restore all customers. The measurement must be more customer-oriented. When the electricity goes out, the customer needs an estimate of how long it will take to turn it back on. This is especially crucial for a small business customer. If we tell him four hours, he may want to send his twenty employees home. A bad estimate will hurt this customer. Sometimes the estimates are unreliable because we deliberately make it longer to protect ourselves. So an important part of reengineering is getting our people to understand the impact of our estimates, and to make them with the customer in mind.

Define your standards and objectives from your customer's point of view. They'll be impossibly ambitious as a result, but in striving to meet them you may well achieve the "impossible."

Ron Rittenmeyer: We had a problem with cut cases. The way the system works is that a salesperson places an order for X number of cases. That order comes into the plant and then they have three days to manufacture it, put it in a box, load it on a truck, and deliver it. The goal is to have it in the store within four days. Well, if you can't fill the order completely, you cut some of the cases out of it. Salespeople also have the right to call in twenty-four hours prior to delivery and add product on. If they do that and you cut it, it still counts as a cut.

Cases get cut for a lot of reasons. You are out of raw materials. You are out of packaging material. You have equipment failures. You messed up the order. Whatever the reason, a cut case is an unsold case.

We talked to the people at our Kirkwood, New York, facility and told them we wanted to lower the number of cut cases. They set up a meeting with the salespeople and educated themselves on the problem—what it meant to the salespeople, to the stores, to the consumer who couldn't find chips for her picnic.

Well, those employees came up with a challenge: They weren't going to cut one single case. They redesigned the way they did the work. They organized laterally so that everyone shared the responsibility; from the time the order was received through its on-time delivery, they worked as a team. Someone who had never worried about packaging material was now making sure there was enough in the plant. The folks who did the loading were making sure the manufacturing equipment was running smoothly.

That plant did something that had never been done before at Frito-Lay: They went seven months without cutting a case. They reduced their costs at the same time. It took what I would call a superhuman effort, but they did it.

Be skeptical of the "may the best man win" mindset. In this context, that means resisting the temptation to define work processes and responsibilities so as to set one unit in competition with others. Our customers demand that we be one company.

Dave Sanders: There were a lot of hassles in the way we were organized. Let me give you a particularly glaring example. There were times when we did work on one side of a street, while the other side, which had the same problem but was in a different geographic division, didn't receive the service. Can you imagine how those customers on the wrong side of the street felt about Detroit Edison?

Part of the problem was that budgets have been allocated by division, and not every division received the same amount for the same project. One manager might have resources, while another might not. No one will officially admit this, but sometimes there has been reluctance to share resources—during a storm, for example. Storms are unpredictable, some areas have more problems than others. The attitude was: "If I share with you it's going to take away from my division's performance."

To address this issue, budgets are now set up according to the type of work needed, rather than by geographic dimension. We're able to share dollars and personnel more freely, putting people on overtime during an emergency and moving them around to the trouble spots. People are now working with their former competitors. Sometimes that's not easy. But it's the best way to get customers' power restored quickly.

Define your goods and services from the point of view of what the customer wants, not from the point of view of what the company can do.

Dave Sanders: One of our key processes is installing power at a new site. For a long time we scheduled it based on our ability to perform, namely when we can get around to it, when we have the right crews available, when the weather is good— all of which lead to excuses and rescheduling. The attitude has been that this is okay. But it's not okay for a customer like McDonald's, for example, which is trying to establish a restaurant at a location faster than its competitors. That type of customer doesn't give us a lot of lead time. We need to connect them when they want to be connected, not at our convenience. We've worked on this and reduced the process from forty-five days to about fifteen days. We want to get it down to three days.

To accomplish this, we've reorganized the people responsible for hookups into a single organization. Before, they were organized in function groups based in the company's six geographic regions. Although these functions were well-defined and well-meaning, they weren't focused on the question "Are we doing it the best way?" As it turned out, the procedures in one region were substantially different from those in another. Our larger customers often did business across several of these divisions, and told us the way we were operating was crazy. They were right. Under reengineering we are developing an organization that operates consistently across our entire service territory.

MEASURING

Performance measurements inevitably get bent, sometimes out of recognition, to support the internal status quo. Remember always that the ultimate measurement is customer satisfaction.

Ron Rittenmeyer: In the past our measurements were much more internal. We measured things like the amount of oil in a product, the amount of moisture, the color of the chips. All of those are important. However, we didn't measure things that the consumer thinks are a heck of a lot more important, like defect appearance. When you buy a bag of chips, you don't want to open it and see a gnarly looking chip. Our thinking was: "Hey, what's one or two less-than-perfect chips?" We didn't think they really mattered. Unfortunately, we'd never asked consumers what they thought.

The same with delivery. We measured everything as a percentage. If a salesperson ordered 1,000 cases and we delivered 995, we called that 99.5 percent compliance, which we thought was pretty darn good. However, when he ordered those 1,000 cases, if we didn't have certain items in stock, we just took them off the order. He might have ordered 1,000, we knocked off 200 and then we delivered 99.5 percent of that, or 796 cases. We think we're doing great but the salesperson is sitting there saying: "Wait a minute, I ordered 1,000 cases, I only got 796, how can that be 99.5 percent?"

We were measuring ourselves with our own set of rules, all of them focused internally. That attitude went through the whole organization. When we started looking at it, it became embarrassing.

Measuring customer satisfaction can also be an effective way to keep managers in touch with the marketplace.

Jim Kutsch, vice president and chief information officer, AT&T Universal Card Services: We seek feedback directly from our customers through random calling. We ask them what their experience of UCS has been like, and what areas could be improved. Our executives visit cities and towns across the country and have dinner with cardmembers, or occasionally invite them to Jacksonville to find out what they think of our product—again, these people are chosen at random.

Each time we talk with the customer, it is a moment of truth—and this is as true for an associate on the telephone as it is for an executive with a focus group.

Linda Plummer, senior manager of Customer Relations, AT&T Universal Card Services: We have many ways of hearing from our customers. We have written surveys; a customer contact group which calls over 1,000 people per month; and a Customer Comments program whereby our associates can record the responses, both positive and negative, that they receive—of course, with the customer's approval. We review the comments and whenever an associate is mentioned favorably, I will write them a 'World of Thanks' note.

If you're measuring personal performance, be sure that you ask the people who know.

Rick Zaffarano, director of Warehouse Operations, Hannaford Brothers: Peer review is another part of our reengineering strategy. We grade team development, applied learning, safety, quality, and customer satisfaction. The rating scale is 1 to 5, with 5 being highest. Peer review is threatening to many. I speak from experience, because I always request a review of my own performance. I want to stand as a model. If someone is consistently scored at 2, the team will deal with that member as a personnel problem. Peer review is the only employee assessment we do.

Reengineering does not mean anarchy. With increased control comes increased accountability—the self-managed performance must be measured. And different measurement techniques are required. The old four-page review form is history.

Marc Swartz, facility director, Hill's Pet Nutrition: We think we have an excellent employee-evaluation process. It starts with the selection of an evaluation team, which includes two members of the evaluated employee's team, his team leader, and one member of a team on either side of him that's either a customer or supplier. So you've got a cross section of people who know his work from different vantage points.

This team then sits down and evaluates him on willingness to learn, quality and quantity indicators, team spirit, absenteeism, cooperation, and any other areas they feel need exploring. Now, the supplier might be thrilled with his work, and his team leader less so, because they see him from a different point of view. All this is discussed and a consensus is reached that balances positives and negatives.

At this point the employee is called in and he receives his evaluation, which is presented in a positive light. We want people leaving the evaluation room feeling good about themselves and wanting to correct any deficiencies that have been pointed out. If you come down too hard on someone, all you're going to do is put a big chip on his shoulder.

Every single individual in the plant, including myself, has a written performance agreement. Once a year, everyone sits down with his team and team leader and writes an agreement as to what he will achieve in three major areas.

The first area is specific deliverables. An employee might agree to be the person on his team responsible for developing a sanitation schedule, or be in charge of preventive maintenance, or responsible for tracking downtime on a given piece of equipment. Each of these clearly defined deliverables has a concurrent improvement goal. So not only will he track downtime on the extruder, but he'll lower it by a minimum of 35 percent. He draws up the schedule, reviews it with the quality systems manager, and trains every member of his team on ways to meet that goal.

Specific deliverable is worth 25 percent of the performance agreement.

The second area is a statement of the specific training an employee will undertake. Every single person in the plant has to be recertified on the fork truck every year. The same goes for first-aid skills. We also have what's called the Drake Safety Training Program: It's a self-taught review of safety concepts that everyone is required to take annually. In addition to those three areas of required training, someone might say: "I'm going to learn how to program PCs so that my team has that added skill." Terrific. Obviously this voluntary training has to be in a useful field, so consultation with the team leader is called for.

Training accounts for 50 percent of the performance agreement.

The third area is behavioral. There are certain behavioral

skills that are part of every job definition—leadership skills, communication skills, consensus-building skills, ten in all. The employee agrees to perform at a minimum acceptable level (level 3)—on a scale of 1 to 5—in each skill. At the end of the year he is rated by his team on that same 1-to-5 scale. If he fails to reach his minimum acceptable level in three of the ten categories, he goes into a performance-improvement process.

The behavioral measurement accounts for 25 percent of the performance agreement.

This agreement is the basis for evaluating an employee's performance for the year. If he fails to live up to his end of the agreement, he becomes ineligible for a bonus.

Performance-measurement processes should be designed on the assumption that people have the potential to do the new work. These processes should be supportive, not punitive.

Kirby Dyess, vice president and director, Human Resources, Intel: We've changed our employee discipline procedures and made employees more accountable. In the past, managers felt frustrated when an employee wasn't performing well, yet many avoided direct confrontation. If they had to reprimand or terminate somebody, they'd bring an expert into the room to make sure they didn't say anything wrong.

Today managers are encouraged to lay out performance standards up front so that employees have a good sense of what's expected of them. If an employee doesn't reach that standard, the manager may suggest they both do evaluations of his or her work and then get together and chat.

Most employees are tougher on themselves than managers are—they have hands-on knowledge and can better judge their suitability and performance.

The manager and employee complete their separate evaluations and get together. It can go one of three ways: The employee realizes it's not the right job for him or her and leaves the company or looks for another job within the company; the employee asks to be redeployed; the employee realizes he or she hasn't been performing at his or her best, and enters into an improvement contract with the manager, or the employee and the manager agree that a downgrade in job scope is appropriate. In the last two cases, we will support him and give him all the training he needs.

We find that by putting the ball in the employee's court, the commitment level rises and employees own their "employability" so that forced terminations can be avoided. In all cases, there are options, and, if additional training is required, it is made available.

A truism: Measurement and reward processes must reinforce the culture you want to create.

Jim Abolt, vice president of Organization and Management Development, Frito-Lay: Our performance management systems incorporate a 360-degree evaluation process in which managers get evaluated by their customers, their peers, and the teams who work under them.

Last year, this process identified one of our most promising managers as being somewhat manipulative and controlling. Six months later an executive level job opened up; under the old system, he would have gotten it. Instead, the position went to a person whose feedback showed him to be more in sync with our reengineered culture.

We let it be known throughout the company why this manager was bypassed for the promotion. It's amazing how quickly people change when they realize their career depends upon it. You can talk about reengineering all you want, but unless that talk is coupled with a change in your evaluation process, you aren't going to see results. Today, this process includes not only results, but the manner in which they were achieved. The point is, the ends don't always justify the means.

COMMUNICATING

Communicating the reengineering message begins with presenting the case for change—letting people know the "why." Then they must be told the "what" and the "how"—the specific impact on their lives.

David Adams, assistant vice president of Corporate Quality, USAA: When reengineering, the biggest challenge to management is to use communication to lessen the threat, to reduce anxiety. We've tried to create a widespread understanding of exactly why we decided to change a prosperous, relatively smooth-running company. We had to drive home the idea that today's success guarantees nothing for tomorrow.

Pattie McWilliams, vice president of Life and Annuity, USAA: In the past, if we were talking about making an organizational change, we wouldn't discuss it with anyone but management. Once we decided, we'd go out and dump it in everybody's lap. We didn't do that this time.

David Adams: We started this process by sharing the results of customer-satisfaction surveys with employees. The surveys showed that while most customers were basically satisfied with our service, a significant number felt there was room for improvement in certain areas. Through informational meetings and newsletters we informed each and every employee that we were going to institute changes with the goal of improving customer satisfaction.

Kenneth McClure, senior vice president of Sales and Marketing, USAA Life Insurance Co.: We wanted to distill our mission into a single statement and we came up with "USAA Life Insurance Co. is here to help each member and his or her family get the life, health, and annuity products they need throughout their lifetimes."

To live up to that mission statement to the best of our ability was the "why" of our reengineering effort.

David Adams: Once people understood the "why" of reengineering, the next step was to articulate the "how." A lot of times people announce that they are going to reengineer, but can't explain what that means; distilling the process into clear language is a big stumbling block to success.

We tried to accomplish this by telling every employee exactly what the change would mean to him. PRIDE (Professionalism

Results in Dedication to Excellence) began in the spring of 1991 with a four-hour course giving an overview of the reengineering process. Employees then broke into smaller groups for a more detailed and specific discussion of how their jobs would change.

Kenneth McClure: Once people really understood, in terms of their day-to-day work life, what reengineering is all about, things started to fall into place. The big picture has to be broken into individual brushstrokes. It all comes down to communication.

Pattie McWilliams: I talk to my employees and my management team every chance I get. I'm very up-front and tell them this is new, we're trying it, we're all in this together. I tell them about my own doubts, my own fears.

The new communications flow can be threatening to many middle managers, who need to be shown how sharing knowledge can be in their best interest, too.

Kirby Dyess: The information explosion has led to some redefining of managerial roles. Historically, managers hoarded information, controlling its release to bolster their power. Those days are over forever. Today we have corporate-wide E-mail. With the push of a button I can send detailed information to everyone in the corporation. In addition, many employees subscribe to news services that come through their PCs automatically every morning. In some cases, employees have access to more information than their managers do.

Take the case of one of our managers whose job is narrowly focused on a support role. Recently we decided that we needed his employees' skills dispersed to the actual business units. Now this manager has his subordinates sitting on the staffs of business-oriented organizations where they have access to a lot of current information about the corporation. They are better informed than he is and that can put him at a disadvantage. I told him that the reason he felt so uncomfortable was that he no longer held all the information and couldn't ration it out. It took some time, but he came to accept this new reality.

No communication process is too humble, or too grand. So use them all, from the simplest (conversations) to the most sophisticated (televised talk shows, with the CEO as moderator).

Ann Monroe, senior vice president of Human Resources, Blue Cross of California: Before we reengineered, intracompany communication was terrible. The many layers of management made consistent communication very difficult. It's like when a line of children whisper a message to each other. By the time it reaches the last child, it's a very changed message.

Today every manager must have a staff meeting, and a one-on-one with every direct report, at least once every two weeks. These are two-way meetings, a chance for the manager to update his people on new developments, and a chance for employees to share ideas and problems.

Every quarter the chairman meets face-to-face with all management in the company and walks through the financial and operational status and upcoming challenges. In this same meeting, management staff discuss the changes that have been made and the results of those changes.

We also have specific "communication vehicles." One is the *Chairman's Report*, a publication that comes out at least once a month, but more frequently if needed. It addresses organizational issues, health-care issues, anything we think people should know about.

Another vehicle is our employee newspaper, which features a lot of hard company news, such as how our sales are doing in this or that area.

A third communication vehicle is an electronic bulletin board called the Grapevine. The Grapevine can get news to every office in the state in an hour. Say there was an article critical of the company in the *Los Angeles Times* in the morning, we could put the article and our rebuttal on the Grapevine and defuse any potential negative impact it might have.

The point is to keep a constant dialogue going in both directions.

Knowledge is power, as the cliche has it. But knowledge is not easy to come by. You earn it by thinking. And all we have to

*think about is information. So make sure that the information
"gets around."*

Ron Rittenmeyer: People by nature want to contribute, and
to make decisions. But that's very difficult to do if they don't
have information, or if they have information but don't know
what to do with it. We went through a very long process that
trained our employees from the bottom up in basic math. This
was followed by a more advanced course that explained what all
the numbers meant. We made information very accessible. We
taught them how to use computers and made them readily available.

One twenty-five-year employee computed the amount of corn
we waste in making Doritos. He was shocked. And he went
ahead and came up with half a dozen ideas to decrease the waste.

ONE MORE DANGER: YOU CAN'T SEE IT

One caveat as you work on your management processes:
Reengineering the Corporation talked about operational processes—processes that have a tangibility, a physicality to them.
We can see them in our laboratories, manufacturing plants,
warehouses, and service centers. By fundamentally changing
them, we can produce radical improvements in our business performance that show up with relative immediacy on our bottom
line. We like tangible things, so as managers we are inclined to
spend time and energy on them.

But management processes aren't always so tangible. We can
see some of their manifestation in measurement reports, in communications media, and in behavior—but the output of these
processes and their effect on the bottom line are not always so
immediate. And because they are hard to see and don't provide
the immediate gratification of results, we sometimes lose our
interest in living in their redesign. Beware: We need more discipline to do management process reengineering than operational
process reengineering. Even our colleagues may not know that
we've stopped working on them until our change initiatives
come painfully to a halt.

CHAPTER 10

WHAT KIND OF PEOPLE DO WE WANT TO WORK WITH?

It seemed so much simpler in the days of the old corporate "machine": You hired people to work for you. So you chose them, judged them, and rewarded them for their ability to perform a specific task.

That doesn't work anymore: Reengineering demands that we hire people to work with us, as part of a community of shared aspirations, ideals, and trust. The ability to perform a specific task isn't enough; today we need people who add value to every process they touch, and who bring values to our company.

The management processes of choosing, judging, and rewarding have to be reengineered to recognize this change. Each process must become a reengineering tool in its own right—and the core of the covenant we managers have with our larger community.

Twice last summer I read some disturbing comments, one by a consultant, the others by journalists, on different aspects of this revolution we're going through. They convinced me once again that reengineering still has a long way to go before it becomes routine.

The first comment concerned Levi Strauss & Company's values statement, a forthright document that reflects the personal convictions of chairman and chief executive Robert D. Haas (great-great-grandnephew of founder Levi Strauss) and his senior management team. His "Aspirations Statement," as it's called, commits management to foster and embody the following sorts of behavior:

• "Directness, openness to influence, commitment to the success of others, and willingness to acknowledge our own contributions to problems."

• "A diverse workforce (age, sex, ethnic group, etc.) at all levels of the organization."

• "Greater recognition—both financial and psychic—for individuals and teams that contribute to our success . . . those who create and innovate and those who continually support day-to-day business requirements."

• Clarity "about company, unit, and individual goals and performance. People must know what is expected of them and receive timely, honest feedback."

• Greater "authority and responsibility of those closest to our products and customers. By actively pushing the responsibility, trust, and recognition into the organization, we can harness and release the capabilities of all our people."

These values sound to me as though they'd emerged from good reengineering thinking: nothing out of the ordinary for any company that wants to join the revolution of our times. Yet you wouldn't know that from the sneering apparel-industry consultant quoted in *Business Week*: "The company has the P.C. [political correctness] mindset," he said. "The Haases think they talk to God."

The second disturbing remark came from *Forbes*, in commenting on the layoffs at Chevron Information Technology Corporation, a subsidiary of the $41 billion petroleum conglomerate. In November of 1993, the magazine reported, all 2,300 of CITC's technology workers were abruptly informed that technological advances, chiefly the rise of the personal computer at the expense of mainframes, had put all their jobs in jeopardy. It was consoling, no doubt, that perhaps 1,800 employees would be able to find new jobs in the restructured company. But that left a good 500 workers, while awaiting their severance, to contemplate just how they'd been treated. "Needless to say, we're completely stressed out," said one dazed worker. "Not a lot of work is getting done. Most of us feel this could have been handled better."

The editors of *Forbes* disagreed with the worker. They thought the layoff communications had been handled just fine. "Hardheaded?" their article concluded. "Yes, but probably realistic."

Neither of these comments surprises me. Both reflect a widespread belief in the business world, especially in North America, that the "hardheaded" way is usually the "realistic" way, or that paying attention to such people-focused matters as social values and aspirations is "soft," "unrealistic," or worse, "P.C."

This belief is either naive or, more likely, just another alibi for grimly holding on to the past. Why? Because people-focused cultures are not merely "nice" things to have if you can afford them. They're not just "nice" at all, and "affording" them is not the issue. In the era of Smooth Sailing, after all, many secure, market-conquering corporations could afford such policies, and didn't buy into them. It's only now, when businesses are recognizing their dependency on people—especially as they reengineer their work processes—that they find themselves forced to get serious about the values and behavior of all their employees.

The testimony of leading managers on this score is positively deafening:

- "You've got to trust the workforce. If you don't, you've done an awfully bad job." (John H. McConnell, chairman and CEO, Worthington Industries)

- "All corporations dream about . . . initiative, but seldom get it. The reason: Too many controls and too much supervision stifle the people on the scene. They feel restricted, intimidated, or bored." (Wayne Calloway, chairman and CEO, PepsiCo)

- "It's not a platitude to say that you have to utilize people's brains and imagination and dedication. They know their jobs better than you do. The fellow running the lathe in the factory knows more about that part of the process than the bureaucrat in the office." (Lawrence Bossidy, chairman and CEO, AlliedSignal)

- "People: the only long-term competitive advantage." (Harley-Davidson, Inc.'s 1992 Annual Report)

- "Our success depends on high-performing people working together in a safe and healthy workplace where diversity, development, and teamwork are valued and recognized." (Weyerhauser Co.'s 1992 Annual Report)

- "People, products, profits. . . . If we take care of our people, products will be created, and profits will follow." (Jerry Sanders, CEO, Advanced Micro Devices)

- "Take care of our people; they, in turn, will deliver the impeccable service demanded by our customers, who will reward us with the profitability necessary to secure our future. People-Service-Profit, these three words are the very foundation of Federal Express." (*Manager's Guide*, published by Federal Express)

Now I'm not naive, either. I'm aware that even in the nineteenth century there were times—around Christmas, say, or at retirement ceremonies—when truly "hard" captains of industry (Scrooge himself, perhaps) could be heard mouthing such sentiments as these. There's a basic truth to them, a truism, in fact, that every manager must acknowledge: Even a corporate machine needs people to be part of it. Without people, there would be no business.

Nevertheless, the logic of the new era we're trying to do business in lifts these sentiments far above the level of truisms. They are truths—"hard" truths, if you will—that no manager can afford to ignore any longer. It wasn't idealistic notions of political correctness that inspired Levi Strauss's Haas to issue the Aspirations Statement, just as it wasn't idealism (or self-pity) that prompted the CITC worker to complain that his company's restructuring could have been better managed.

Does the apparel-industry consultant object to Levi Strauss's commitment to ethnic and gender "diversity"? Let him look around at America's changing population, please, or at the composition of the world market for jeans. In this context, diversity is not only an ideal, it is a practical, urgent necessity.

How far does *Forbes*'s celebration of "hardheadedness" at CITC go? As far as risking the morale of the workers who remained after the layoffs? Probably not. Yet the moral of a brutal restructuring—"It could happen to you"—isn't likely to escape any of CITC's 2,300 employees. In today's business world, you don't flout Federal Express's injunction to managers to "take care of our people" without eventually paying for it—literally, on the bottom line.

The logic of new times, revolutionary times, is behind people-focused management. In the old days of machine-like corporations, "management" was a small, coherent group of relatively educated men. "Labor," by contrast, was a vast, uncohesive (unless unionized) group of relatively uneducated men *and* women, often of different ethnic groups. It may have made sense, then, for managers to ignore how workers thought and felt and behaved toward customers, the company, and each other. For the vast majority of managers, in most industries, it hardly mattered what their employees' "values" were, as long as they did their jobs according to contract. Unions went along with this attitude. They helped management design the work rules that adapted labor's muscles to the corporate machines. And as for workers' values, they were happy to take on the responsibility for teaching them.

This tidy arrangement simply doesn't work anymore. Conditions have changed too radically. In most American industries today, the only social-status differences between managers and their employee "associates" are created by income, not by class or educational background. In technology-driven or talent-driven industries, in fact, the "background" distinctions may favor the employees, who are often better educated and credentialed than their managers. They are also, many of them, better paid than all but the top managers. Even in industries less obviously glamorous than electronics or apparel, reengineering has made businesses increasingly reliant on the skills, imaginations, commitment, values, and behavior of their employees. It has also transformed their employees' work, giving them more authority, and the work more content, interest, and complexity.

What's happening, in short, is the breakdown of the two "great divides" that used to separate management from labor: the background divide of education and social class and the foreground divide of utility to the business. In most industries today, at least in the developed world, the old distinctions no longer apply.

The fact that they don't apply is having a momentous impact on the way managers now have to *live* one of the great questions on their professional agenda—what kind of people do we want to work with? This question contains many others. If we know what kind of people we want to work with (and we do—they are not human machine-parts; they are the people who can do reengineered work), how and where do we find such people? Who should be the judge? How do we do the judging? Can we train or educate the sort of people we already have to be the sort of people we want to have? How do we pay these people?

Let's begin, as reengineering insists that we must always begin, with the goals we want to achieve, the desired *results*.

THE NEW WORKFORCE

According to the Taylorite logic of the corporate machine, employees were judged as useful (or not) solely in terms of how well (or poorly) they performed the particular mechanical skills they brought to the workplace, or learned on the job. You were deployed, paid, awarded bonuses, promoted, demoted, fired, and so forth, for the work you did. Indeed, from the managerial point of view, you *were* the work you did.

This has always been true in some sense. But while pre-industrial forms of production identified us with a whole "trade," and thus a whole way of relating to the world, socially and economically, modern production has seen to it that employees are identified much more narrowly with a specific function or tool in a purely quantitative process. People were hired to fill *slots*. In the corporation-as-machine you are Mr. Two Hundred Turns of the Wrench per Hour, or Ms. Two Hundred Thirty-five Cold Calls per Day. This process of assimilation—people to machines, machines to people—is still going on wherever it is believed both possible and efficient. In health care, for example, it was never believed possible. Now it is. Whether it will also be believed effective remains to be seen.

In many industries, however, the historical trend toward machine-tooling the workforce is being reversed. As work changes and customers become more demanding, more knowing, more elusive, it's no longer good enough for the people on the value-adding chain to fill *slots*. Consequently, employees are being substantially *dis*assimilated and *dis*identified from the narrow, quantifiable functions they perform. They are being reconceptualized as fully human beings capable of bringing far more to the struggle for markets than merely technical skills.

This new historical trend is what I call the socialization of the workforce—including a large part of management. *Socialization*, as I use the term here, means the developmental process of learning to relate positively and constructively on a broad range of tasks with a broader range of people. Yes, I know: We're all supposed to have been socialized by our families, teachers, friends, and neighbors, well before we ever come to work. Once on the job, however, our socialization often comes undone when we find ourselves mindlessly involved in mechanical work processes or bureaucratic management processes. We regress. But today, in industries all over the world, even the most mechanized workers and bureaucratized managers are, by necessity, being reintegrated into the increasingly demanding (and in demand) *social* aspects of contemporary work lives. My friend Warren Bennis, who for years has studied and written on the subject of management and leadership, describes the kind of person we *now* want to work with as a "deep generalist." He means a person who is broad enough to respond appropriately to shifting work demands, to changing market opportunities, to evolving products and services, and to the ever-pressing demands of customers, but who has gone deep enough into some area of expertise to bring a well-honed and valuable skill to the enterprise.

To put it bluntly, when it comes to hiring people to work with, people who can do reengineered work, *we want it all*. We want the expert all-'rounder, the team player who can work alone, the good student with street smarts, the numbers person who speaks with eloquence, the people person who is also a technocrat, the self-confident follower who is also a leader who listens. In developing a hiring policy today, managers can't afford *not* to be greedy.

Consider what the (pseudonymous) ABC Company had to learn about hiring. ABC used to screen prospective employees by sending them home to study detailed job descriptions, then testing them on what they had remembered. There was nothing wrong with this so long as the job descriptions were an accurate representation of what would be asked of the employees once they were actually on the job. As soon as the representation ceased to be true, however, the hiring procedure ceased to be meaningful.

With the end of the Smooth Sailing years, most such job descriptions are no sooner written down than they cease to be true. Technological developments falsify them, new competitors with new products or services falsify them, new government regulations falsify them, *change* falsifies them. Moreover, what I've called the *social* aspect of work performance is notoriously difficult to describe, and, at least in any conventional sense, equally difficult to test for. When work becomes highly cooperative, urgently demanding, customized and personalized, what's the point in asking a candidate for a sales job to go home and study, say, a life insurance policy, and then test him on how he'd sell it? There is no point.

Let me put the difference between hiring processes then and now in the most chilling way I can think of. Today, *it's not only what you know that counts, it's what kind of person you are.* What kind of person you are means, essentially, whether you'll be able to live up to, or at least aspire to, the "values" both social and work-related that I listed in Chapter 6. To determine the answer to that question, the hiring process must pose a whole range of other questions to and about the candidate. And as with values, so with these questions, I've found great commonalities across all sorts of businesses and industries. Reengineering employers want to know about:

• Your ability to communicate. Can you be clear about what you want and need? Can you be persuasive, or even eloquent—in selling situations, in teamwork, in service situations? Can you teach or mentor others?

• Your interpersonal savvy. Can you trust and respect people of different backgrounds, ethnicity, or religion? Can you work with women? With men? Are you a good judge of character? Where are you on the trusting and trustworthy scale, the mutual- and self-respect scale, the aggression scale, the honesty scale, the cooperation scale? How well do you deal with the unexpected in other people's behavior? How well do you deal with so-called personality or political problems? By working around them, confronting them, finessing them?

• Your self-confidence. Can you make decisions? *How* do you make decisions—impulsively or deliberatively? Can you take initiative? Can you ask for help? Can you give help?

• Your resourcefulness and adaptability. Are you self-reliant? Reliant on others? Or (preferably) both? Are you nimble in mind and body, but steady in character and personality? What's your instinctive response to change? What's your educated response to change?

• Leadership qualities. Can you listen, really listen? Can you speak so that others listen, really listen? Can you win authority from others, and delegate authority to others? Can you judge and reward the people you work with on the basis of their performance, and their performance alone?

Occasionally, on my trips out into the field, I get a certain kind of "hardheaded" question about the scope and weight of the demands and expectations that reengineering is placing on employees these days. "What's the point of looking for the same sort of qualities in a forklift operator that you look for in a warehouse manager," this question goes—"or, for that matter, that you look for in a division manager?"

The question might come straight out of the Smooth Sailing, "machine"-corporation years. Look into the mind's eye of the man who asks it: You can practically see the forklift operator with long steel tines growing out of his arms. Still, the question deserves an answer, and the answer comes from how the qualities of leadership, self-management, and teamwork must interrelate in reengineered work *and* management. For forklift operators, *just as for everyone else in the company*, the pivotal demands are a knowledge of the total work process in which they're engaged, and a commitment to the excellence of its people and products. These demands call on what we often call "teamwork." You can't work well with a team without some degree of leadership ability, and a large degree of self-management capacity. Listen to Marc Swartz, facility director at the Richmond, Indiana, plant of Hill's Pet Nutrition, as he tries to explain his company's hiring policies. He uses the three concepts—teamwork, self-management, leadership—almost interchangeably.

One of the reasons that the bar continues to rise on employment here is that we're learning what is really needed to be successful here. We're looking for a very significant degree of, if not proven capability, at least capability to learn to be a leader. When we say self-managing, we don't mean the day you come to work, we mean the ability to become self-managing. That means the ability to give feedback to your peers, to manage performance across the team, to manage individual performance, to manage absentee problems—in other words, a significant number of the kinds of issues that the manager would handle in a traditional organization. We expect teams and team members to handle these things. So you're looking for a different person here altogether.

Another argument I get on my visits to companies undergoing reengineering is that there just aren't enough people with all these sterling qualities to go around. No doubt this is true in some markets, perhaps in many. But managers do their businesses no favors by *assuming* it's true. The assumption is too convenient an excuse for refusing to reengineer. "Oh, we couldn't possibly do anything so radical," I've heard people say. "The workers around here won't change. They balk; they're culturally so different."

When I hear this, my advice is always the same: Test the assumption. Test it during the hiring process, test it in your training and education programs, and test it in practice. Then, if the assumption proves correct, test your management.

In the end, what I'm saying comes down to what I said before: Be greedy. It may be a while before your workforce (or managerial force) is fully socialized, but demand more than your share, insist on more than you can "reasonably" expect. You've got to have it.

Now let me show you some ideas about how to go get it.

EDUCATING

I'll start with education because the most frequent people-related question I get in my discussions with clients concerns the educability of *current* workers and managers in the ways, means, and goals of reengineering. The fashionable term for that sort of education these days is *reskilling*, but the word is too narrow and mechanistic for me. "Skills" suggests special technical, knowledge-based abilities; it does not suggest broad social (or cultural) behaviors, nor does it suggest general managerial abilities. As for the "re-" in "reskilling," it seems to me to point us away from the best, most beneficial assumption we can make about our workers and managers: namely, that they all possess, within themselves, the resources of mind and character that they need *to learn*. Only one word describes the process that depends on those resources—education.

We've all gotten used to the idea that managing might just as well be another way of saying educating, training, teaching employees, including the managers themselves.

Technological change, broadly speaking, is driving this need for teaching, as it always has. Corporations, even the corporations of the Smooth Sailing years, had to train incoming workers to submit their bodies and minds to the discipline of their machines. It hardly mattered whether the machines were made of bureaucratic paper or of iron and steel, few workers knew from the start exactly how to serve them—how to fit themselves into the available slots. Moreover, in the course of time, the machines changed. Managers would tinker with the bureaucratic machines, engineers would tinker with the metal ones, sometimes replacing them with entirely different machines, and the corporation consequently would have to retrain their employees in the new routines and services. Laying them off was undesirable. First, we had a covenant with them, usually based on their and our continued good performance; second, they still knew a lot about the business and its culture; third, the changes were never very radical.

Technological change still drives education processes today, but with two differences. The first is that the change comes with a disruptive relentlessness that used to take decades to play itself out, and now takes only years or months. The second difference is that our concept of technology is opening up to include managerial issues.

Culture is probably the most dramatic of these issues. Time was, not long ago, when people believed that a culture, even a business culture, was a *given*. Like the weather, it was something you couldn't do anything about. Now when managers speak of their business's culture, as often as not it's to talk about changing it, using it, manipulating it in some way—to better serve the business. Culture has become a tool.

This expansion of the concept of technology has expanded, as well, the concept of education. Managers used to be able to tick off their education obligations to their people pretty quickly: so many hours of upgrading on the machines, so many hours re-routinizing managers on some new administrative procedure. That was the end of it. Culture, values, teamwork and leadership development, social skills, resource development—these things were either taken for granted, left to emerge "naturally," considered irrelevant, or dismissed as "soft." They certainly weren't things to be taught.

Now they must be, just as much as, or more than, the "hard" operational skills like running a lathe. Consider, for example, the education and development that AT&T Universal Card Services give their employees. It is extraordinary, yet in some form also mandatory. Bob O'Neal, senior manager for Universal Card University, describes "three learning areas where we need to provide leadership."

The first one is people's ability to do their job. We provide that to all the people who work here. The second thing we try to do is communicate and reinforce our company's values, vision, and mission so that people will know what we believe in. Not only how to do the work but in what philosophical framework we expect it to be done: how we expect each other to interact with our customers; how we expect that we will interact with each other; what our relationships with each other are; and so on.

That's the cultural piece of our training, and it begins at the beginning. The whole recruitment process teaches people who we are as a company, and how we interact. Right off the bat we treat the people we are hiring as customers, letting them know what's happening with their applications, keeping them posted on their test appointments, and things like that. We treat them as we would like to be treated, yes, but also as we want them to treat customers.

Then we put successful applicants through a two-day orientation program, which gives them an opportunity to learn not only about us as a company but also about themselves as individuals. They get to compare who they are and what they're looking for with this company they're about to join. It's an opportunity for them to explore what will make them successful with the company.

In Bob O'Neal's account, you'll notice, it might almost seem that, under the heading of education, cultural matters are pushing out skills training. I doubt that this is actually so, however, at AT&T Universal Card Services or anywhere else. Acculturation techniques are new, and newly vital, but they are additions to the old managerial skill-training tasks, not substitutions for them. There are two reasons for this, one obvious, the other not so obvious.

The obvious reason is the fantastic pace of change in *what has to be done*. I'm not talking now about any kind of technological change, only about what we're called upon to do with the technologies we already have. Think of health-care insurance, for example, a head-spinning industry if there ever was one. Ann Monroe, senior vice president of Human Resources, Blue Cross of California, told us that to avoid problems in claims settlement, billing, and premium collection, they not only had to put their people through a training program in the basics of health-care financing, but they had to keep training and retraining them. "Health care in this country is in a period of rapid change," she said, with the result that Blue Cross's ongoing skills training has to involve "lectures, workshops, and various 'communication vehicles' such as newsletters—all aimed at keeping our employees on top of what's happening both within the company and in the health care field in general."

The less obvious reason for education goes to the heart of the emerging new social contract in American business. Michael A. Weiss, vice chairman, The Limited, Inc., put the employer's side of it in the simplest possible terms: "We . . . show you that we value you by helping you develop your career." But from the employees' side, as Charles Handy reminded us a few years ago, careers nowadays have to be portable if they're to be worth much. It's no good signing up with a company, even for what amounts to a career-development course, if the course leads only to the next step, and the next, within the same company. This is especially true in violently change-prone or high-risk industries, where management can promise little more than a term of employment—on a product-development project, say. But even in more stable industries and companies, employees these days are well advised to keep their eye on the ball; that is, to keep adding to their own portfolio of marketable personal assets. "We show you that we value you," Weiss might have said, "by helping you add to your value in the labor market." And the best way to do that, still, is to add valuable skills. The assets gained from cultural training—learning the social virtues of teamwork, customer relations, and getting along with people different from oneself—are increasingly recognized as vital assets in anyone's portfolio, for any sort of job. They are skills that often get the foot in the door in a new field.

Federal Express, as longtime employee Everett Meadow told us, "is a company that rolls out the red carpet to you and says, 'Be all that you can be.'" Meadow himself started in an entry-level position; thanks to his having taken advantage of FedEx's training programs, he now works in data network support.

But "be all that you can be," the old army recruiting slogan, for many people means "be a manager." This wasn't always the case. Even in America, the land of opportunity, workers often found it difficult to imagine themselves becoming managers. Like Sergeant Warden in *From Here to Eternity* (Burt Lancaster in the movie), they felt the weight of huge ideological, class, cultural, and (often) ethnic differences holding them back from reaching for "officer" status. To cross that divide was more of a temptation than it was an opportunity. They might "rise," but at the cost of betraying those they left behind.

This is no longer the case. America's great achievement in the last fifty years or so—and reengineering's achievement more recently—has been to open up managerial status, rewards, and responsibilities to everyone. Reengineering's role has been to insist on the bottom-line rationale of self-management and team-work, and of circulating knowledge, and bearers of knowledge, from the bottom up.

Putting all this together, companies are now faced with new incentives to provide their people with opportunities for management education. FedEx, with the founding of its Leadership Institute in 1984, which provides management training, may have gone farther, faster, in this direction than many other corporations. They also, no doubt, hit the snag faster, as Anne Swearingen Duty, manager, Employee Communications, explained:

> Several years ago, we noticed what to us was an excessive turnover rate among managers within their first year: About one out of ten was either quitting or being terminated. We did a survey among the departed managers and found that the problem boiled down to the fact that they weren't prepared to step into a managerial role. This led to us starting an interesting and unusual training program called LEAP—Leadership Evaluation and Awareness Process.
>
> LEAP begins with a course called "Is Management For Me?" Employees who are thinking of moving into management get the real lowdown on the joys and headaches and responsibilities of a managerial job. The class also covers managing in a reengineered environment—listening skills, team building, sensitivity to diversity. After an employee has made a firm decision to go into management, her peers answer a questionnaire rating her leadership qualities. The final step is a panel interview, during which a team of three senior managers assess whether the candidate understands and can apply the leadership dimensions that are the foundation of LEAP. Successful candidates are "endorsed," meaning they may now apply for management positions. They don't automatically become managers.

But the point of LEAP may not be in the details. The point is that FedEx, in the face of significant evidence that their management-training program was not working, resolved to fix it, to *make* it work, not to dispense with it. They see their responsibility, and their opportunity, to be that great.

PAYING

Compensation has lately become the most controversial of all management processes. This is unfortunate because the controversy has focused attention on what is probably a less important aspect of the issue—remuneration for CEOs. Far more interesting are the changes in payment practices brought about, in part, by reengineering.

Reengineering's contribution to the pay process is easily stated. Reengineering insists that people no longer be paid the old way, for the time they put in as appendages to the corporate machine. Instead, they must be paid for the value(s) they add to the business. Reengineering also insists (though perhaps with more force than originality on this point) that payment practices can and should be used experimentally, boldly, subtly, as a management tool for change and the reinforcement of change. Change, that is, both for the benefit of the individual and for the benefit of the larger organization of work.

The best example of the latter is the bifocal attention that reengineering wants to bring to bear on individual and on team performance. How do we devise payment schemes that encourage teamwork without discouraging individual responsibility and initiative? Or vice versa? The answer, in most companies, seems to be that you don't—at least not with base pay. You do it with incentive pay, such as bonuses and stock options. Ira Walter, director of Compensation, Benefits, and Human Resource Information Systems for AT&T Universal Card Services, described for us the bare bones of their pay scheme:

> The essence of our program is divided into two components. One is our base pay, which is fairly typical. We value the worth of every job based on market conditions; that's a fixed cost. Then we have a rather rich variable pay program which is contingent on business outcomes.

The key variable at AT&T Universal Card Services is quality, as monitored *daily* on more than 100 different processes.

But the key distinction is between team and individual performance.

The question is, though, "What's a team?" And it's not an easy one to answer. At AT&T Universal Card Services, for example, Walter says, "For pay purposes we define team at the company level. Every non-management employee has a relatively significant amount of money riding on quality results of the team." Indeed they do. "If the company makes quality [scores 96 out of 100 on the performance measures]," Walter continues, "each and every day of the quarter, every associate will earn a bonus check of 12 percent of their salary for that quarter. If there are 90 days in a quarter and we make quality in only 60, they'd get two-thirds, or 8 percent of earnings."

But I'm not sure we've gone far enough in our thinking on this score. If teamwork is a truly integral part of the reengineered workplace, it may not be a good idea to link it to an "extra," even one as important as extra pay. The message could be that teamwork is an extra, too. Still, linking it to incentive pay is what companies do, and the reports indicate that it's working well.

At Rick Zaffarano's Hannaford Bros. Co.'s warehouse, for example, incentive bonuses are allocated on three levels—the warehouse operation as a whole, the "team" as described above, and the individual. This is a fairly common solution, where circumstances permit, and a good one (subject to the reengineer's constant need to invent a better one, of course). But it's not the division into three levels that matters most with Zaffarano's plan, or always with reengineering; what really counts are the values and behaviors that the bonus process rewards:

> One bonus is based on our budget, and is computed annually. If we hit our budget, there is a certain payout, and if we improve on it, the payout gets better. This is the first year there is no cap; previously it was 10 percent of salary. That is, we gave 5 percent if we made budget and 10 percent if we beat budget. Now, because we've been getting really aggressive on our budget, it's 6 percent at budget, and no limit if we beat it. So if we have a $10 million budget, and come in at $8 million, we'll share in that $2

million we saved. The total payout for an associate has been usually around $3,000, but it could be more this year, or less. Generally, they've been averaging around 9 percent, so they've been doing really well. At bonus time, we have a day of celebration with a big rally. It creates a lot of enthusiasm.

Individual incentives are a payout based on efficiency of performance. We pay on performances that exceed the norm. Then we have a team incentive plan. We operate on throughput, which means so many pieces in, so many pieces out. We have broken it down and customized goals for each team. So all the hours the team works, divided by all the pieces they handle, totals out to a certain number of pieces per man hour. If they exceed their goal, the team gets an incentive sum.

The pay process is not a reengineering *tool*, really; it's a tool kit. Indeed, a catalogue of all the instruments in an entire tool kit, many of them invented in the last few years, would make a thick book. That book will only get thicker, as new tools are developed to cope with the accelerating change in the workforce, the decline of unionism, and the ever-increasing urgency of new customer demands. Nevertheless, the constant in the process will remain: the need to ask questions, openly and constantly. How better to target values with incentives? How to juggle individual-based pay with team-based pay? How to define "team" for pay purposes? What's the right proportion of base pay and incentive pay? How far can a company depart (up or down) from the market rates for work? What are the right pay differentials in a company? (Right for what? Morale? Morality? The Market?) Like everything else about reengineering, these questions are never answered with finality.

HOW DO YOU CHOOSE NEW EMPLOYEES?

Just as pay processes offer a reengineer a wide variety of tools, so do the processes involved in selecting and hiring new employees. We aren't looking for "slots" anymore; we can't afford them. So our screening, interviewing, and testing of potential employees needs to be based on their ability to contribute to a reengineered community—how likely are "they" to become a productive part of "we"?

The key to choosing processes is the same as it is with the pay processes: open questions, constantly asked, based on how close your desired results came to what you actually accomplished. Let me show you how I've seen it work.

Screening

In many U.S. and European communities, managers are in a buyer's labor market, so they can afford to do a quick screen of job applicants, often initially on the phone. But Marc Swartz of Hill's Pet Nutrition uses phone screening to find out more than a prospective hire's past work history; Swartz probes for values:

> Let me give you an example: If you ask somebody the question, "What did you do last summer?," and they say, "Well, I built an addition on my house." You say, "That's interesting, tell me how you did that." They say, "Well, my father is a carpenter, so he came over and helped me do the carpentry work. And I have a real good friend who's a plumber, so he and I put the plumbing in together. And I didn't know anybody who's an electrician, so I really had to hire the electrical work."
>
> What kind of behavior do you hear in that description? You hear teamwork, willingness to use resources, ability to learn. It's the kind of behavior you would want in your plant. As opposed to, "I had a pretty easy summer, I did a little lifeguarding, but basically hung around and didn't have a whole lot to do."

Interviewing

The face-to-face interview remains the indispensable hiring tool, but how useful it can be depends on the thrust of the questions and the judgment of the interviewer. The interview used to find the kind of person they want to work with at Aetna Life and

Casualty, as Hardy Mason explains, manages to hit on just about every one of the expectations that reengineering companies have of prospective employees these days:

> We are careful to use a behavior-oriented approach. We would say, "Explain how you made a certain recommendation to management, and then persuaded them to accept something unprecedented" [*communications ability*]. Or we would say, "Describe how you resolved a difficult conflict between yourself and someone you work with" [*interpersonal savvy*]. Or, "How would you give feedback to an employee whose work is disappointing?" [*teaching ability*]. Or, "Tell me what you'd do if you were caught between an angry customer and a boss who could help you but can't stand bad news" [*ability to confront*]. Or, "Have you ever asked for a raise? If so, how did you do it and what did it feel like?" [*self-confidence*]. Or, "When was the last time you felt your authority challenged, at home or on the job, and how did you handle it?" [*leadership ability*]. Or, for managers: "Do you own and use a word-processing computer?" [*adaptability to change, self-reliance*].

Note that the interview is *itself* a rigorous test of the candidate's communications skills and interpersonal savvy—not to mention, memory, imagination, and general mental resourcefulness.

Interviewing Plus

One of the most exhaustive hiring procedures I know of was developed by Corning Inc.'s Blacksburg, Virginia, manufacturing facility. Famous for its ceramics substrates (they're used in automobile emission control systems), the Blacksburg facility needs employees with good technical and scientific expertise, but just as important it needs people capable of teamwork. Norman Garrity, a Corning executive vice president, who established many of the workforce norms at Blacksburg, told us what happens after the candidate fills out the usual forms:

Applicants come back for a two-and-a-half-hour interview, which reveals their communications skills and attitudes toward work. Applicants who pass this stage are tested for math skills (needed to deal with the plant's statistical process controls) and writing skills. We ask them to write an essay about the most important person in their life. You might be surprised at how much a discerning reader will discover from this essay. Finally, we put them into a team setting to see how well they function at building consensus without a supervisor present. If the applicant has a family, the company invites that family in to learn what kind of work is done at Corning and the type of stresses people encounter there. The company is aware that the family's reaction has a lot to do with the employee's eventual success or failure on the job.

Every step in this procedure was carefully worked out after Corning's leaders studied hiring stratagems in companies all over the world. Of the 8,000 initial applicants interviewed at the Blacksburg plant, the company hired less than 400, or one out of 20. The results have been impressive. In six years, only one employee has left the division and only one has been discharged. This unusually stable workforce has broken productivity records and made the division one of the toughest competitors in its world market.

"What If" Exercises

Some companies put prospective employees through elaborate role-playing exercises. Some are designed to reveal how the person might behave on his own—in relation to an unusual customer demand, say, or a breakdown in customary procedures. Others are designed to test the candidate's ability to get along with others. Marc Swartz describes an exercise that probes both these issues at the same time:

We'll give six people a written problem. Fifteen minutes to think about how they want to respond, and then 20 minutes to role-play. The problem goes like this: One of your team members, Bobby, misses work every other Friday. Now you don't know for a fact *why* he misses work, but you do know that he has a son who's a senior in high school and is a championship wrestler. Wrestling tournaments are every Friday. How are you going to handle the problem?

Some people say, "Well, that's real obvious. The guy is going to a wrestling match, let's just fire the bum." Others say, "It sounds like Bobby has a problem. We better sit down and find out what's happening. Susie, will you do it? Frank, will you?" Which sort of person would you want on your team? Or what about the one who says, "I'd like to take a few Fridays off, too. Let's just let Bobby slide through and maybe I can slide through later."

The point of this exercise is not to ferret out the people-pleasers, whose careless ways might cause trouble down the road. The point is to have a discussion about team responsibility, and the balance between homelife and worklife, in which even those with the right attitude will learn something.

Peer Participation

In the old days of "machine-tooled" employment policies, the job applicant went to the union hiring hall, the personnel manager, or the human resources office, and was measured for his or her "fit" in the available "slot." If the fit was okay, the candidate was sent on to fill the slot. Beginning, middle, and end of story: call it "Untouched by Human Hands."

Well, in the reengineering corporation, hiring is no longer a question of finding the right-shaped pegs for given holes. What's being offered and applied for, sometimes unbeknownst to the applicant, is something much more like a membership. It's not just a job that is at issue; it's a certain kind of *belonging*. Belonging, that is, to a work team . . . to a human, value-adding process.

As a result, many companies have come to believe that the hiring procedure is too important to be left up to "the experts"—the personnel or human resource people. If it's true, as Lawrence Bossidy says, that the lathe operator knows more about his side of the business than anybody else, it should also be true that he knows more about the kind of person he wants to work with than anybody else.

Note, however, that I say "should." It's not always the case that people do know what's good for them—or, more important, for the business—when they consider what kind of people they want to work with. (The reasons for this, and the corrective for them, I'll discuss in a moment.)

Still, peer participation in the hiring process is a growing trend in the reengineering corporation. Not determination, mind you, participation. And even with that qualification, many companies insist that employees get some training in hiring judgment and techniques before they participate. One such company is Hill's Pet Nutrition, as Gordon Walter, Human Resources manager at the Richmond plant, explained:

> Anyone who wants to be involved in the selection process has to take and pass a workshop. Targeted selection principles are taught, along with interviewing techniques. It's a two-day workshop. It enables someone to be qualified to do telephone screening, and then to graduate, if you will, to doing interviews. They sit in as observers, then they practice, and then actually do interviews under supervision. Then, if they want to participate in the [final] assessment centers, they must get more training, go through more practice sessions, and be certified. Once someone has that certification, he or she has equal say, actually, with any of us [HR people]. Their voice and input counts just as much as any of ours.

Peer participation in hiring is today commonplace only around CEO levels; at floor and field levels it is a distinctly minority practice. But it is likely to grow. It will grow not out of any democratic ideals but out of the most practical discipline of the free market. Today, and for the foreseeable future, people-management has to be largely a process of engaging the workforce, enlisting them heart, soul, and mind in their work. What better way to do it than by giving them a voice in whom they should work with?

What About the People You May Not Want to Work With?

The great flaw in peer participation in hiring is that people tend to want to work with people who (they think) are like themselves. They may not want anyone who is much better than they are at the job. They may not even like it if anyone is much worse, though this is more rare. And they may want someone of the same background, ethnicity, and gender.

These prejudices are commonplace. They are also seriously dysfunctional. No manager can afford to risk a return to the old union-inspired tyranny of the "work-rate," the "work-rule," the dead "normal" performance. Top performance, excellence, is now required of everyone.

By the same token, no manager can afford a homogeneous workforce. Not only is imposing one against the law, not only is finding one an impossibility in most communities, not only does encouraging one contradict most companies' values, homogeneity is also extremely bad for business.

Racial, religious, ethnic, gender diversity, on the other hand, is demonstrably good for business. It is good for business, first, because no business can any longer afford to ignore the business of any large group of people—never mind either of the two major genders. (No doubt there are still some gender-based businesses, but it seems like only yesterday that there was an absolute rule that women didn't buy cars and men didn't buy cosmetics.)

But the business argument for diversity goes deeper than this. We need different perspectives to solve the problems of the new work. Diversity of viewpoint creates the best solutions, but we need reengineered management processes to release the workforce imagination and creativity, which let diverse viewpoints flourish.

Some companies, by necessity, are a lot further along in realizing this than others, like FedEx, as Roger Easom tells us:

Many of our operational areas have a very diverse ethnic makeup. Some [other] areas have a preponderance of one ethnic group far more than the general population. How do you deal with a team that may develop racial or ethnic friction? How to be sensitive to different religious or cultural attitudes? Managers often face some huge challenges.

Just for an obvious example, take a white male manager whose work group—representative of the local community—is predominantly black and 40 percent female. That manager has to learn new ways of seeing, hearing, and understanding. He'll find problems he never suspected, problems he wouldn't have if everybody in the work group were just like himself. [FedEx feels they must try] to train him to deal with diversities, not as negative, problem-causing things but as factors that can be directed in a positive way.

Within FedEx, the Diversity Training Program is famous—and quite popular. Linda Edwards, senior manager/management preceptor, Leadership Institute, explains:

The course is mandatory for officers and directors. [As for others], we have a waiting list that stretches ahead for a whole year. Some people are probably sent by their management because they've had personnel difficulties, but most people are volunteers. The most common reasons I hear [are]: "I need to learn how to deal with African Americans," or with women, or with Hispanics. Then I have to explain that that's not what this course is about. We don't try to explain people anthropologically; we want to teach an understanding of people as individuals.

One of the most frequent problems I see in my class is that of the male manager in his work relations with women. I often hear, "I feel so unsure of how to deal with them that I always make sure my door is open whenever a woman is in my office." What does that reflect? The man is totally on guard. He's worried that if he does or says the wrong thing he's going to be in trouble—and so he's defeating his whole purpose as a manager, which is to counsel, coach, and develop employees. We have to make man-

agers perceive that women and minorities shouldn't be treated
with kid gloves but with realism and understanding.

WHATEVER HAPPENED TO THE SOCIAL CONTRACT?

The Smooth Sailing era, as far as employment went, might just
as well have been called the Golden Age of the Social Contract.
Just as all French, Germans, Japanese, and Scandinavians enjoyed
a *politically* underwritten social contract with their governments, so many Americans in that era enjoyed an *economically*
underwritten contract with the companies that employed them.
The deal was not unlike what existed, as we've seen, in utility
companies like Arizona Public Service. If you worked up to the
norm ("the rate"), you had a job, a salary or wage, and benefits
guaranteed for the rest of your working life.

Of course, workers would face periods of unemployment
during downturns in the business cycle. But most of those laid
off could look forward to getting their jobs back when the market for whatever they produced ticked up again. There were
probably always more ambitious managers in any given company than there was room for at the top, too. But managers
could always choose to leave for bluer skies. Meanwhile, markets were expanding and margins were getting more and more
comfortable. Everyone worshiped growth, and in return growth
spread its blessings far and wide. Jobs, benefits, perks of all
kinds fell upon American managers and workers. Thus, despite
the great strikes of the era, some of them violent, the days of the
Smooth Sailing were a time of harmony between Americans and
their employers—the harmony of a comfortable security.

As shown, all this began to come to an end after 1973. But
the storm did not come up suddenly; seas just got rougher and
rougher. At many businesses, in fact, the calm of hard-earned
security slipped away without anyone's really noticing it. And
when managers did notice it, many clung, as we've seen, ever
more desperately to business as usual.

Many argue that the social contract is a thing of the past. In
the U.S., it is said, no companies are ever again going to be able

to offer their employees anything like the kind of job security, salary raises, and benefits they used to offer. In Europe and Japan, it is said, governments are forced by taxpayer revolts to abandon much of the social-security legislation that is the groundwork of their contracts with their people. There's some truth here. Companies around the world are finding it difficult to pay for social services, while companies in our country may never again be able to afford the cost of the old contract—or want to. But this is not to say that the social contract, on this continent or any other, is a thing of the past. It is only to say that the social contract will never again provide quite the same peace and comfort as it did (or as we merely remember it did) in calmer years.

Layoffs, for example: the grimmest sign of our revolutionary times, especially for managers and technicians. Remember the story of CITC. The myth would have it that the best that companies can now offer prospective employees is something like the following: "We cannot guarantee you a job forever, not even for the next five years, but we can guarantee that however long you stay with us, when we lay you off, we'll do it in such a way that you'll want to come back—if we ever have a job for you to come back to."

This is not much of a deal.

In fact, however, companies will be able, and forced, to offer much more than that. At the least, they will have to offer "No guarantees, but _____ " contracts. The blank will then be filled in with all sorts of worthwhile *quids pro quo*—training, education, contacts, humane and interesting work, and so forth; plus salaries, profit-sharing, stock options, and benefits that will be substantial, if not quite so rocket-like as they were in the 1980s.

At the best, many companies will be able and obliged to offer their core workers and managers deals right up there in value with anything seen in the 1980s. This is as certain as anything can be in our tumultuous world. The whole emphasis on *people*, as one of the most important competitive advantages a company can create, demands that top management attract, cultivate, and keep the best workforce they can possibly find. There is no more vital investment, so they will make it.

Now, on whatever end of this spectrum your company might fall, let me give you a model contract to illustrate the choices of mutual representations a company and its people may make. It's not intended to be a "legal" document, of course; instead, it sets out the values in which everyone can place trust:

We, the company, will use our best efforts to be:

- Aggressive in the pursuit of new ideas, new services, new products, and new markets—and, of course, new customers.
- Diligent in the pursuit of a culture of willingness.
- Better and better and better in the work that we do—both our operational and management work.
- Fair, equitable, and open in our relationship with people.

Our intent is that our business grow and prosper, and as it does, it is our intent, to have work for our people—even as we learn to do our work better and better. This, of course, must be consistent with maintaining strong business performances and producing a good return to our investors. If we should find that we must reduce our workforce, for any reason whatsoever, we shall treat our people with dignity and respect.

While a person is part of this company, he or she will be paid fairly on the basis of individual performance in adding business value to the company, and on the performance of the company.

And while a person is part of this company, we shall provide him or her with opportunities for personal development and challenging and meaningful work.

I, the employee will use my best efforts to:

- Contribute to the development of new ideas, new services, new products, new markets, and new customers.
- Utilize my skills and capabilities in the service of our customers.
- Participate in a culture of willingness.
- Do my work and help others to do their work, better and better and better.
- Be fair, open, and equitable in my relationships with the people of this company.

In return for fair pay and the company's investment in my development, I will do my work with quality and excellence and will use my best efforts to personally develop to serve the needs of the company, its markets, and its customers.

You can see that in this "contract" there are no guarantees. In fact, there is a tension between the company's interests, the employee's interests, and the investor's interests. An enterprise will run best when all of these interests can be aligned—but, again, the reality of today's business conditions dictates that *there be no guarantees*. And, of course, this contract is not intended to have legal weight. But it's not legal weight that matters most today; what matters is moral weight, the values expressed, the clear intent that everyone will use their best efforts.

Now, you may not agree with all of the terms in this example—so, change them to fit your business, your culture. I'm not holding this out as being universal. But my advice is to be clear about your covenants with your people. At a minimum, agree to jointly live the questions of purpose, culture, process, and people.

CHAPTER 11

CASES IN POINT—HOW WE CHOSE

Hiring and firing, the age-old managerial prerogatives, are being tamed now by a new tool kit of processes, and by a new covenant between a company and its employees.

To prepare myself for this book, I visited and talked with managers and workers at hundreds of companies. Among other things, I wanted to see how managers were living the "people" question. Many were stuck in the past, using controlling practices based on an antagonistic relationship with employees. Sometimes they had adopted a new language—empowerment, for example—but their methods remained the same. Government regulation was often blamed for their inability to change.

But hearteningly, a number of companies have adopted human resource practices that follow the principles of reengineering. These share four important characteristics:

• First, the job of "human resource management" has moved to the frontline. Self-managers and process- and people-managers have taken responsibility for these matters. They may get help from a human resources staff, but the new work demands frontline authority and accountability for educating, hiring, measuring, and compensating employees.

• Second, these people practices are imbued with strong cultural values of honesty, trust, and respect.

• Third, open communication and knowledge-sharing are cornerstones of their design.

• Fourth, they are based on appreciation of human potential, a conviction that when people are freed from the limitations of narrow, fragmented jobs they are capable (with education) of full ownership of the new work.

Over the next several pages, I want to share with you examples of these practices and processes. Not everything you read will be right for your company—change must be tailored to your purpose, culture, and operations. But these testimonials do serve as evidence that part two of the reengineering revolution is well under way.

EDUCATION

The demands on process- and people-managers are heavier than ever. Here's one description of what's required.

Kirby Dyess, vice president and director, Human Resources, Intel: Managers have to have some well-developed qualities in order to succeed in Intel's highly volatile and intense environment. They must have very strong networking skills. They must be able to go out and ask people the right questions. They must align their goals with those of the corporation. They must have a big-picture perspective to see how the pieces fit together. They must be good coaches with a real sensitivity to people. They must be open to criticism. They must be thoughtful and deliberate. They must know how to hire people who will work well together.

After determining leadership potential, formal education begins. Leadership skills can be taught.

Mike Parrish, vice president and general manager, Nucor: In the past we promoted people into supervisory roles without giving them much leadership training. We'd pick people from the ranks who were good at what they did and got along well with people, but there was no formal training. We are currently planning a seminar program especially for our old-line supervisors, who see their responsibility as getting as many tons of steel out the door as possible. We want them to understand that getting the steel out is their crew's responsibility—their responsibility is to take care of that crew. If they do, the tons will get out. Today's supervisor might have to deal with someone who's unhappy about his vacation schedule. That's a people problem, one they may need extra training to learn how to handle.

Education should include an understanding of fellow employees' work.

Mike Parrish: We try to utilize our employees to their fullest capabilities. For example, we sometimes take machine operators and match them with maintenance people, so they get a chance to learn something of each other's trade. It helps people to mesh, to see that everything that goes on in the plant is interrelated. Attitudes have improved—operators used to say that maintenance people didn't do a good enough job, and vice versa. Walking in somebody else's shoes lets you see things through their eyes.

In changing marketplaces, education must be continuous and extensive.

Ann Monroe, senior vice president of Human Resources, Blue Cross of California: In our claims business, we take in $2.4 billion a year and pay out $1.7 billion. Paying those claims correctly is absolutely critical. And it wasn't happening. Neither were things like collecting premiums owed and accurate billing.

As we began to research the problem, we found that our own people didn't understand health-care financing. That was quite an eye-opener. I think management often takes it for granted that frontline employees have some knowledge of the business. That's a mistake. Nothing should be taken for granted. If all someone's been doing for ten years is simple billing and they have no knowledge of the complexities of health insurance, they're simply not going to be equipped to do a good job. Billing for medical procedures is very different from billing for screws and washers. There are endless variables depending on the doctor, the patient, the hospital, the policy itself.

So we went back to square one and instituted a training program in the basics of health care financing. We didn't expect people to become experts, but we did want them to have an overview, and to understand specifically how interrelated billing, collections, claims payment, and medical treatment are. Now people aren't working in a vacuum. They know that if a claim comes in and it isn't paid correctly the first time, all sorts of problems are going to be created, problems that just keep snowballing. We expect them to do whatever it takes—consulting with other units, using technology, contacting the providers—to get it right the first time.

This training and communication is an ongoing thing, as health care in this country is in a period of rapid change. We learned the importance of keeping our employees on top of what's happening both within the company and in the field in general. And now we're seeing the payoff.

Reengineering's emphasis on employees' values and behavior is far from being "optional," but neither does it substitute for technical ability. You've got to know how to do the job.

Carole Waite, business leader in the Small Business and Select Markets Customer Business Unit, Blue Cross and Blue Shield of Massachusetts: What qualities would I want on my ideal team? I'm looking for people who have a mature attitude and some common sense. People who aren't afraid, who don't whine, and who are willing to say "Let's go for it!" Mature, enthusiastic, down-to-earth type of people. I don't care if they're 23 or 93.

There are people whose behavior is wonderful but they can't do the job. A team leader and I did a review on an associate last week and we agreed she was a great person but she wasn't quite up to the job. When we told her, she said: "How can you say that about me? I'm such a good team player and so nice." We had to explain very gently that, yes, her attitude was terrific, but she was going to have to keep working on her skills.

Teaching is a way of showing people how they are connected—to their peers, their products and services, and their customers. Often, however, the people we hope to teach turn out to be the company's best teachers themselves.

Dave Sanders, director of Business Process Reengineering, Detroit Edison: One thing we've discovered is that people feel disconnected from what happens outside their own sphere. Sometimes they know who gives them their work, they may know who they give work to, but this is about all they know. They don't see the big picture, or their place in it. They lack connection to the end product and to the customer.

So we're doing some process mapping to help people understand how things work around here, what makes things happen. This must be done in a clear and detailed way, so that people can grasp it. An abstract flow chart is so remote from their daily concerns that it's meaningless. To better reflect reality we interviewed the people who do the work, such as linemen, field foremen, and dispatchers. They helped create the document. In the past, this was done by third-level managers, who would either write about how it was twenty years ago, when they were out there, or how they thought it should be today. They were out of touch.

As a result, we've not only got a more realistic map, we've also unleashed some ideas. We have a lot of people in the company who can make an impact. They know things about their jobs, their tools, and their work which can help the company, but they've had an ingrained idea that it's not their job to make suggestions or fix their own problems. The attitude has been, "When are 'they' going to fix this problem?" Now people understand that they themselves are "they."

During our interviews, we came across some interesting ideas and initiatives. For example, some people have taken it upon themselves to enter changes on field prints early, as opposed to waiting until the work is done, cutting weeks out of the usual process of distributing this information. This is saving money and increasing efficiency. We want to know about these things, we want everyone's suggestions.

Enlightened personal development benefits both the employee and the company.

Kirby Dyess: We have a sabbatical program that gives all employees including managers as much as three months off every seven years. In order to leave on sabbatical, you have to have someone who can step into your shoes for that period, and so you do some cross training to get that person ready. Filling in for someone on sabbatical is a wonderful way for managers to broaden their skills. In fact, many people use it as a springboard to change jobs within Intel.

A lot of people think of the sabbatical system as an advantage for the employee, but we have found it to be an advantage to the corporation because it forces employees to cross-train a successor.

Reengineered work brings about structural changes that may be more difficult for managers than workers. Don't assume that managers will need less support. They may well need more.

Kirby Dyess: Intel has had some experience with the problem of redeploying human resources, and we have found managers to be the toughest group of people to redeploy. They are used to their own organization. Let me give you an example.

There was the manager of a large customer-marketing operation who had about 90 people reporting to him. He was used to working within a well-established hierarchical structure. Well, when we reengineered we made changes in his product line, adding a very successful training program for the distributors.

The need for his marketing function disappeared. It wasn't adding value, but it was adding costs.

We redeployed the employees and then came the time to redeploy this manager. He was experiencing a lot of anxiety about his place in the company. First, we reassured him that there was a place for him, that he was valued. Then we gave him the chance to do a great deal of soul searching, to ask himself who he was, where he wanted to go, what he really wanted to do. We always give managers this opportunity during a transitional period; the introspection is very valuable. Self-knowledge will help a displaced manager find his place in our reengineered environment.

He used some of the tools we provide to help our managers during this period. He talked to an outside consultant we provided. He used the online program that is available in our Employee Development Centers; using a series of cross-referenced questions, it helps you determine where your interests and skills lie. He also talked to a manager in Human Resources, who was able to give him a fresh perspective on his strengths, weaknesses, and options. This support network lessens managers' anxiety during this painful redeployment process.

After examining both himself and the company, this manager moved into a start-up organization. He went from having 90 direct reports to having two. This created a new set of challenges. He was used to being on top and managing from that perspective. In a start-up, you have to let go of all that, roll up your sleeves, and get involved in every aspect of the business. All of a sudden he had no secretary. This created not only practical problems, but ego problems. We have people you can talk to about personal issues, and some pretty robust PC classes to deal with the practical. After he got past the initial lessons, he jumped in with both feet, has become an expert and is doing incredible things with the PC.

After eight months, this man was running a strong, focused business. To me, that kind of adaptation is exceptional. It's not easy to take what looks like a big step backward. Many managers balk at the prospect. At Intel we try and make a difficult process tolerable by breaking it down into a series of definable steps.

Educating managers to cope with new situations often requires all the developmental resources that a company can bring to bear.

Kirby Dyess: When a manager is preparing to take on a new job at Intel, we make a strong effort to connect him or her with people within the company who can provide coaching.

A specialist at Human Resources will talk to HR people in different departments to try and track down someone who can provide just the right kind of insight and direction.

These matches are usually pretty successful because learning goes both ways. I use myself as an example. Before taking this position, I had been running start-up businesses which employed a handful of people. I had a lot to learn. I used my predecessors as a resource, plus several people I was hooked up with who literally acted as day-to-day coaches. I basically made a contract with them; in exchange for their help, I gave them my fresh perspective on the organization. They have been incredible resources for me.

Through this coaching and support network, no manager is thrown into the water without a life jacket on and an experienced swimmer by their side.

Like every process, enabling demands constant education in values, education that must be carried out at every level of the company—especially, perhaps, at the management level—if it is to achieve its goal.

Mike Lamar, assistant vice president, Property and Casualty Operations Analysis, USAA: We weren't happy with readings we were getting from our customer response surveys, so we instituted PRIDE (Professionalism Results in Dedication to Excellence) in 1991, with the aim of continuous improvement in the quality of service. PRIDE has introduced work teams to USAA, which resulted in no small amount of confusion and readjustment.

Del Chisholm, assistant vice president of PRIDE: We were so anxious to get the program started that we bypassed our management staff. We went right to our first line employees and said: "We want your ideas, we want you empowered, and we want you to act as teams." They came out of training all fired up and ready to change the world, and ran smack up against a management staff which was still operating by all the old rules. We said, "Whoops, we made a mistake here. Let's back up."

Mike Lamar: We hadn't made it clear to managers that they had to evolve from controller to coach, from supervisor to supporter, and from administrator to enabler.

Del Chisholm: The managers stormed into PRIDE offices saying: "What! These people want to organize committees, take actions and carry out projects? What am I supposed to do?" Meanwhile, employees were getting frustrated by this managerial resistance. When confronted with enormous change, managers experience personal and psychological reactions that can't be underestimated or overlooked.

Mike Lamar: We tried to make them understand, in numerous meetings and one-to-ones, that the reason for all the change was simple: To improve customer service. Once they saw that everything grew out of that principle, they calmed down. Although there was some restructuring as a result of PRIDE's efforts, no one was fired. Some people were moved to other areas. USAA doesn't want to downsize, we're a growing company and we take care of our people.

A manager's education often and rightly comes from three sources: formal teaching, the help of peers, and the constructive criticism of workers.

Kirby Dyess: For about six or seven years we have actually been having employees coaching their managers. The process starts by putting what I call "subordinate input" into managers' performance reviews. We ask them such questions as: Is your manager a model of Intel values? Is he or she adding value to you and your team? Do you have all the resources you need to get the job done?

We take this input, relay it to the manager, and ask him to come up with a formal development plan to address any problems. The manager will then stand up in front of his subordinates and say: "I heard your input, and I'm not going to change because . . . However, I also heard your input on another problem, and it was good feedback, and I'm going to develop a plan to correct the problem. What I need from you is help via more feedback."

As their role changes, managers must learn to accept the fact that their technical and interpersonal skills, what they actually do, the use-value they bring to the enterprise, are what's important, not their hierarchical rank. During this painful transition, a company has to prepare its managers, support them, and recognize that some people just won't make it.

Ron Rittenmeyer, vice president of Frito-Lay Business Systems: The person who has it hardest during reengineering is the frontline manager. All of a sudden you have no identity. You're no longer making decisions. People don't have to come to you for permission anymore. It's a very vulnerable position.

Dave Zemelman, senior vice president of Human Resources, Frito-Lay: Managers see their careers disappearing in front of their eyes. There's tremendous anxiety. They want to know what their options are.

Jim Abolt, vice president of Organization and Management Development, Frito-Lay: We got rid of 40 percent of the managers in our plants. Those remaining said: "I don't know what I do anymore. What does my career look like?" Looking back, we didn't have it planned as well as we should have, we didn't have a ready answer for them.

If you are going to flatten the organization and not provide people with a new understanding of what their career looks like, you might as well pack it in.

Dave Zemelman: So we rethought what we had to offer our managers. We looked at their career paths.

Jim Abolt: The way you got ahead in the past was by progressing from managing technicians to managing managers. Since we took layers out of the organization, there were very few opportunities left to manage managers. So we moved the emphasis to skills. We said you can still progress in your career by acquiring more skills. We defined those skills as those needed to make our new work environment succeed. Skills like coaching, communication, team-building, anything that will make a great manager in an empowered organization.

We now have some people making as much as $90,000 dollars a year, even though they aren't managing other managers. Some of them still miss having a title and the status that goes with it. The truth is, some managers miss the old ways. Most of those end up leaving the company. Not everybody is going to be a happy camper.

HIRING

Reengineering demands more sophisticated screening and hiring processes. Gone are the days of the simple interview. Here are a set of requirements for these processes, followed by three examples:

- *Develop a profile of the technical and interpersonal skills that the new work requires.*

- *Remember that an ability to learn is one of the important capabilities you are looking for.*

- *Determine what formal testing procedures can tell you about the candidate.*

- *As much as possible, observe the candidate operating under real or simulated work conditions.*

- *Broaden the interviewing process to include team members with whom the candidate would be working.*

- *Don't limit your pool of candidates by requiring past*

experience. It may not be relevant to the new work, and it may eliminate talented candidates.

• *Design the recruiting process to expose your culture to the candidate, and treat her as a company member during the process. The candidate should clearly understand what it means to work for your company.*

Rick Zaffarano, director of Warehouse Operations, Hannaford Brothers: Our 14-member reengineering-implementation team had the assignment of hiring 100 warehouse people. It was a trial. We did an analysis of the type of associate we were looking for, and then created a system to recruit and screen them.

We wanted team players—innovative, creative, and with demonstrated ability to apply learning. We were looking for the ability to resolve conflict—one question we asked applicants was: "You've probably run into someone who really irritated and frustrated you. How did you handle that situation?" We used simulations to observe behaviors. We had three levels of interviews, with different people conducting each one. We were looking for stars.

After the interview data was integrated, people who passed were sent on to a team simulation session. The simulation was based on a game called A-Okay Doorbell. With limits on money, time, and material, the team had to build as many doorbells as they could. They had to buy their materials from a little shop we set up, build, and then sell the doorbells profitably.

The team members didn't know each other. Our observers watched their behavior. Who was solving the problems? Who was taking the lead? What kind of interaction did they have? Were they personable or just blowing each other off? All of this was noted and, finally, there was a debriefing of the observers.

Then, because this is a physical job, we did an intensive physical assessment. The whole process was very intense for the applicants—over eight hours of tests.

To give them an idea of the work environment, we showed them a video. We wanted to be upfront with them. Then they had a final interview, which was actually sort of a reality check, with the director. They could ask any question—with their spouse present if they wished. We really wanted them to pick us, as well as our picking them. Sometimes people would back out at that point, but these were well-paying jobs, so that didn't happen too often.

We ended up hiring insurance salesmen, shoe salesmen, you name it. We went for qualities and potential, not skills in hand.

Later, we had some analysis done of the people we'd ended up with. It determined that the screening was about 90 percent effective. That is, about 10 percent of the people shouldn't have been hired. Interestingly, we discovered that, on the whole, the objective criteria were more valid than our impressions. Most of the time when we judged someone as unacceptable, but the testing rated him or her as qualified, we hired that person and found that the numbers had been more on target than our perceptions.

We felt our results justified all the time and effort we spent on hiring. Our measurement of personnel is based on several factors: turnover rate, inventory accuracy, throughput (numbers of pieces handled in and handled out), speed of handling, accident rate, incidence of damage, percentage of inventory sold, overall warehousing costs—all traditional measurements subject to comparison. Our numbers kept improving.

Linda Plummer, senior manager of Customer Relations, AT&T Universal Card Services: We have an extensive hiring process. It's expensive, but the quality of people we get is outstanding. They're motivated, bright, and when they're hired they feel as if they've really "made it."

We begin with a written problem-solving test, which is not designed for any specific level of education—in other words, non–college grads aren't excluded. Those who pass go on to a role-playing situation: We give them information about a fictitious company, then someone calls and pretends to be a customer. We evaluate this interaction in terms of flexibility, interpersonal skills, and general attitude toward the customer.

Qualifiers go on to a formal employment interview, where we look for such things as stability of past employment, satisfactory work record, and so on. Another interview follows, with an operations manager. We take the candidates through our operations center to give them a feel for the environment.

It is a pretty thorough process—out of 100 people who take the written test, we end up hiring about ten.

Gordon Walter, Human Resources manager, Hill's Pet Nutrition: Employees are invited to participate in the hiring process of fellow team members. We take people right off the shop floor. To prepare them, they're trained in interviewing techniques and methodology.

Marc Swartz, facility director, Hill's Pet Nutrition: Our hiring focus is on people with the ability and willingness to learn, as opposed to skills in hand. The underlying thought is that if the attitude is there, we can "take the mystery out of the skill."

The hiring process begins with the job-seeker filling out a standard Hill's application. This is followed by a basic skills test, which assesses not only present ability, but also learnability, in math, reading comprehension, and things of that nature.

Following completion of those steps, which screen out a significant number of people, the applicant has an hour-long telephone interview.

This interview is followed by a three-hour session at our Assessment Center, which focuses on role-playing in a simulated work environment.

We'll put eight people together, tell them they're the A&B Electric Company, and give them the parts necessary to assemble a circuit board. They also get the price of the raw materials and the price of the finished product. Their job is to manufacture circuit boards, sell them, and make a profit. There's a twenty-minute planning period, a twenty-minute execution period, followed by a repeat of the same sequence. Four people assess their behavior.

We see all kinds of behavior during these sessions. It's fascinating. There'll be the guy who has an electrical background and says: "Okay, fellas, get out of the way, I build these boards all the time. You can figure out what we do with them."

Other common behaviors we see are: hanging back and not saying a word the whole time; being unwilling to get out of a chair and get to work; a lack of urgency. Then there'll be the person who has never built a board and says: "Can we take a few minutes to talk about how we're going to get this together?" That usually generates a response of: "That's a good idea, I'll read the instructions. Can anyone help us understand what these words mean?"

Obviously, that's the person we want in our reengineered organization—someone who displays ability and interest in teamwork.

After successful completion of the Assessment Center process, there are one-on-one interviews with team leaders and peers. These are structured interviews that use predetermined questions. A typical question is: "Tell me about a disagreement with a peer, and how it was resolved. It could be at work, at church, or wherever."

In answering, we don't allow applicants to get away with phrases like: "This is what I saw somebody do." You cut them off and say: "Let me be clear. I want to know what you did in that situation." If they can't answer you, then they probably just walked away from the problem without becoming involved.

What we're looking for is an answer like: "My last job I worked maintenance over at the bus factory. Me and a co-worker were trying to fix one of the hydraulic presses and disagreed on how to handle a safety concern. At first we were kind of arguing with each other, yelling and screaming, but it became real obvious, at least to me, that it was going nowhere. So I suggested that we stop work for a few minutes and go get our safety director and sit down and see if we could just talk our way through it. Which is exactly what we did."

It's amazing how much we learn about a person. Sometimes people dissemble in an effort to paint a good picture of themselves, but after a while you develop a pretty sharp "truth meter," and see through the insincerity.

The entire hiring process takes over eleven hours of a person's time and involves six different visits. So it is a long and arduous process. If they make it through, they know they are very special people in our eyes. This sets a nice tone because the message is: "You are part of a very elite group. We're going to treat you well, but we expect you to do a great job."

Over the last three years we've been able to refine the whole process, as we find out what's really needed to be successful at our company. It's not easy to find good people. We really want self-managing team players. We don't mean from day one, but we have to see the ability to grow into the role. That means the ability to give feedback to your peers, to manage individual and team performance, and to deal with problems like absenteeism. In short, it means handling issues and problems that a manager would handle in a traditional organization.

Everyone you interview should be treated with respect, as you would wish them to treat you and your customers in the event that they're hired.

Bob O'Neal, senior manager, Universal Card University, AT&T Universal Card Services: From the moment an applicant steps through our door, they will get messages about who we are as a company. We treat the people we are hiring as *customers*. That means communicating with them, keeping them informed about how their application is progressing, their testing appointments, anything at all we can do to make them feel comfortable and valued. Even if they end up not being hired, we want the experience to have been a good one.

It doesn't make any sense to reengineer the hiring process, then undercut it with old style seniority or hierarchy.

Rick Zaffarano: If I had to name the biggest obstacle we've faced, seniority jumps to mind. We knew that when seniority reared its ugly head, our system would be in trouble. That sounds strange, since I've said that the people we hired were new to the company. But you have to remember they came from traditional environments, and from a highly unionized area. Most were accustomed to seniority as a rule of working life, almost an unassailable right. We were trying to break all the old rules and busting that one was dangerous.

The expectations about seniority arose from the fact that we hadn't hired 100 people in one day, but 24 people every two weeks over a three-month period. That allowed for the training echelons. So some felt they had seniority over the people who came later, which was scary. But that's the mentality. We were up against the old paradigm, not from everyone, but from a sizable scattering of workers who were really trying to push the issue.

We had seven teams, with roughly 20 people on each. The pro-seniority factions wanted first-comers to get first pick of jobs. But the rest of the team members didn't agree. There was a split and a minor power struggle. From a manager's viewpoint, this is another situation where you're sitting there twiddling your thumbs wishing you could take charge. But again you have to refrain from simply stepping in and saying, "There will be no seniority rules and this is why." Instead, we said, "These are the bad effects seniority can have on your team. Please think them through before you arrive at your consensus."

Our fear was that seniority rules would erode the whole system. They would be a real downer. The junior guy—who was only six months junior—would feel discriminated against. The teamwork would deteriorate when somebody used seniority to avoid doing something difficult, or to defeat team consensus. It would be a retreat to the old days. We realized we had to come up with something across the board that would allow the teams to deal with—and defuse—the issue.

So we formed an hourly employees' committee—no member was salaried, it was all team representation. They thrashed it out and came up with a compromise that, fortunately, was according to our original design—rotation of positions and shifts.

They also created an alternative to seniority that worked for everyone. They worked out levels of prerogative based on how productive an individual was, or how much he contributed to the team effort. The scale was almost like that of seniority, but it was based on performance, which made it more acceptable to us.

PAYING

Compensation programs must support both your business objectives and the culture to which you aspire. Incentive compensation is an important tool. Be careful to keep the performance measures clear and simple so that there is no misunderstanding about your objectives.

Ann Monroe, senior vice president of Human Resources, Blue Cross of California: As we reengineered, we found that we were learning to do a lot more work with fewer people. Layoffs began, but we soon realized we were balancing our books on the backs of the hourly workers. Meaning, no matter how many hourly employees we laid off, we still had the same six levels of managers above them. We put out a mandate saying that we were moving quickly toward having no more than four levels of managers between any worker in the company and the chairman. We wanted to flatten the organization: It was too deep, and that made it difficult to convey information intelligibly, either up or down. And, of course, the many levels made changes of any kind hard to effect.

So as part of our reengineering, we moved a lot of people out of management into individual-contributor status. This entailed making some changes in our compensation system, because an individual contributor could only go so far; you could make more money only by being promoted to manager. For example, you might have a high-level actuary or attorney who worked side by side with the general manager of a large business unit. The specialist was actually as important to the operation as the manager, but could never be paid as much. In order to rise to the salary level of the manager, the specialist would have to have people reporting to him or her. So we made our salary grades parallel. Now, a highly skilled individual contributor can be paid as much as someone who manages people. That took away much of the inducement to manage people rather than projects.

As the company evolved, we needed more people who could manage projects, so we began a series of recognition programs.

Many of those who received top recognition were honored for their project achievements rather than for a supervisory role.

We also put in an incentive plan, which set four different targets. To start with, we set a target percentage for each person—if we achieve our profit goals, you'll get X percent of your salary as a bonus. Targets range from 5 percent for supervisors all the way up to 50 percent for the CEO. Those ex-managers we made individual contributors are included as well, if they are at a high enough level. Then the bonus plan has three different components. First, everyone's bonus is relative to the results shown by the corporate bottom line that year. Second, the bonus is also relative to the bottom line results of the market segment in which they work—for instance, units like individual, small group, or senior products. Then the third component is what we call personal. That includes each person's individual business goals, behavioral goals, and how well they did in managing their people.

In the first years, there were no bonuses. The corporate earnings didn't justify them, nor did the earnings of the business segments. But some units did get in the black, and that quickly drew attention. We tried to identify the key management or business processes that led to their success. We worked the data over and over and over.

As we moved toward a broader organization, we enlarged the span of control. In most businesses, an officer will have eight to nine people reporting to him—that's the span. Some supervisors now have 26 reporting directly. So we broadened spans of control, flattened the organization, and introduced incentive plans tied directly to the business results.

In one of our two major business groups we introduced a combined team- and skill-based pay scheme. The incentive here was to encourage the employees to become more productive by learning new skills because taking on a new skill meant a pay raise. Simultaneously, we placed these multi-skilled employees into defined teams (about 20 to a team) with their own portfolio of business to service and grow. And it worked.

In short, we flattened the organization, increased span of control, added a skill-based pay model, and increased productivity and profit as a result.

You must be prepared to use performance appraisal processes to teach your culture, even when doing so seems unjust. Either that, or rethink your principles and culture. This is an example of living the question.

Jim Abolt: We turned a lot of our assessment measurements upside down. One of our logistics directors—the folks who get the product from the plant to the salespeople—had just had an incredibly dynamite year in terms of the bottom line. He got his performance appraisal from his manager and it was just average. He was told that if he repeated his performance the next year, it would be unacceptable. He was just flabbergasted.

We had to sit him down and point out that, yes, the numbers were terrific, but they hadn't been reached in a manner consistent with the organizational and cultural principles we wanted at Frito-Lay.

He was going around making decisions for other people, solving their problems for them. He established all the goals. He formulated all the action plans. He followed up personally to make sure that those plans were executed correctly. He worked like crazy. Great, but all wrong.

His people didn't know what a cost plan is, they had no grasp of teamwork, no knowledge of company numbers. All they knew was that they were supposed to move this pallet of product into that truck. We weren't going to reward a manager who was stopping change in its tracks. We told him we wanted him to transfer his knowledge to his team, to help them learn, to make his traditional role obsolete. The message was that in the future we were going to evaluate him on how well his team was able to continuously improve. He got the message and ran with it. We have promoted him to director.

THE NEW COVENANT

It's important always to respect the individual—all individuals, but especially those who have put the company good over personal advancement.

Ron Rittenmeyer, vice president of Frito-Lay Business Systems: We asked all employees to examine their operations, to rethink them. When this process began, one of the first things people realized was that they could do the job with less people. This led to the hard issue of what happens to the people you no longer need.

We asked the employees how we should handle the situation. It was agreed that the first line of action would be to not replace people who left. The second would be to reassign people whenever possible. And finally, when a layoff was unavoidable, the person involved would be treated with respect and dignity. There's no easy way to lay a person off, but it's crucial for the culture of this company that it be done with compassion.

Because employees were in on this every step of the way, we avoided a lot of the anxiety and mistrust that surrounds layoffs.

Kirby Dyess: At Intel, redeployment plays a very big role. Reengineering shook everything up, a lot of businesses were cut loose, leaving a lot of managers adrift. We're not about to ignore someone who has done an excellent job, has no performance problems, and, by the way, probably worked himself right out of a job—he is the one who put together the plan that blew up the organization. Since then he's been sweating to find new places for his people.

We don't say to someone like that: "Sorry, you're out a job." We find a place for him.

Employees are more likely to buy into the new covenant if they are allowed to participate in any resolution of disputes.

Armando Flores, vice president of Human Resources, Arizona Public Service: We have an "equity program" designed to resolve issues related to fairness. If an employee has a complaint or dispute involving promotion, discipline, or any other area where they feel they've been treated unfairly, they can take it up with a five-person panel. Three of the people on that panel are their peers, the other two represent management. The panel listens, considers, and then makes a decision. The company stands by whatever that panel decides.

The new covenant is not just about ending the relationship between company and employee with respect. It's an ongoing pact with every worker. It requires living the culture.

Mike Parrish: We recently completed a major project, and how it came about in the first place and then was executed say a great deal about how this company runs. We installed a rolling mill that will allow us to develop a new product—small wide-flange beams. The original impetus came from our sales manager, who saw there was a market for the beams. He and his people looked into the feasibility of the project, talked to customers about it, and eventually we took the idea to a corporate meeting, where it was approved. We decided to put in a state-of-the-art reheat furnace at the same time. It was also necessary to do some work on our caster to accommodate the expected increase in volume. The whole installation took three weeks, during which time we shut down. This was a significant investment—the equipment and shutdown cost about $35 million.

Now, this shutdown posed some problems for our employees. During the year we usually have two one-week shutdowns, one in the spring and one in the fall. Most of our workers take their two weeks of vacation time during those weeks. The one-time three-week shutdown meant that the only people taking home a paycheck would be those who had accrued extra vacation weeks. So we tried to find everyone else at least a week of work here at the plant. In addition, we sent people to our sister divisions for training on the equipment. We even sent people to Italy, where the equipment comes from, for training over there. We always try to take care of our people.

CHAPTER 12

THE SECOND MANAGERIAL REVOLUTION

The first managerial revolution shifted power.
The second will deliver our freedom.

It has been very difficult for people—for managers themselves no less than for other workers and the public—to grasp the dimensions of the revolution going on in business today. Like the proverbial elephant, it's too big for any one person to comprehend. Your neighbor's family touches a piece of it when the principal breadwinner gets laid off from a once-promising job. You see a piece of it when Wal-Mart comes to your neighborhood and Main Street turns into a ghost town. And you yourself touch a piece of it when you reengineer a traditionally organized work process in your company.

Perhaps the best way to grasp what's going on is to think

back to comparable business revolutions in the past. Think, for instance, of the cataclysmic changes that befell American farmers in the 1920s. To most of us, these events are probably best known from John Steinbeck's novel (or the movie based on it), *The Grapes of Wrath*:

> And at last the owner men came to the point. The tenant system won't work any more. One man on a tractor can take the place of twelve or fourteen families. Pay him a wage and take all the crop. We have to do it. We don't like to do it . . .

In our terms, what was happening here was the reengineering of work. But the reengineering of management was not far behind:

> And it came about that the owners no longer worked on their farms. They farmed on paper; and they forgot the land, the smell, the feel of it, and remembered only that they owned it, remembered only that they gained and lost by it. And some of the farms grew so large that one man could not even conceive of them any more, so large that it took batteries of bookkeepers to keep track of interest and gain and loss; chemists to test the soil. . . . And the owners not only did not work the farms any more, many of them had never seen the farms they owned.

Steinbeck was simplifying a complex historical development for dramatic effect, but he was not far off the mark. For some years already, age-old relationships among ownership, leadership, and (let's say) workership had been undergoing the most wrenching changes. And by no means only in agriculture. In fact, the most famous contemporary non-fiction book on the subject, James Burnham's *The Managerial Revolution* (1960), did not even mention agriculture. Burnham's revolution was taking place in the nation's factories, transportation companies, banks, and the like. But it was the same revolution, really, as the one Steinbeck described. The owner who worked at what he owned, often having inherited it from a father or grandfather who had built the factory out of nothingness, that owner-worker was split in two. On the one hand, he became a salaried worker or employee—the machinist or the bookkeeper or the chemist. On the other hand, he became the far-distant owner—or, to speak more accurately, an investor. But this left a big hole where leadership had been. Who was going to supervise the farm, run the factory, or whatever? The answer is in Burnham's title—managers.

All this seems terribly obvious to us; or at least it did. But it was not obvious at the time. Power always has to be legitimated; leadership of an economic enterprise brings with it power: How then could enterprise leaders legitimate their power? Well, worker-owners had been staking their legitimacy on two grounds that had survived challenge since time immemorial: They'd *made* the business or farm themselves, or had at least inherited it; and they continued to work at it. Non-owning managers had to produce something that would replace this. They did. They simply promised that by virtue of their (credentialed) educations, their professional dedication, and their self-motivation, they could run the business or farm more efficiently, more profitably, than the owner-workers could ever do.

This argument won the day. Actually, it was an easy win: Many farmers were sorry to lose their farms, but many, many more were happy to throw over centuries of bondage to the soil for the relative freedom and opportunity of the cities. Likewise, many inheritors of factories and railroads and banks were sad to lose the power and prestige of running such important institutions; but many, many more were delighted to take their money and run with it, free at last. The hard part came with the managers' claims to legitimacy—their promise of greater efficiency, rising profits, and higher standards of living. But who would deny that they had delivered on it? The truth is that the managerial revolution that kicked off the middle years of this century, the years of Smooth Sailing, has been a great success.

But since 1973, something has been happening to the managers' corporations. It's not our fault, exactly. The "something" crept up on us so slowly and deviously, and pounced so randomly, and left so many (other) people so much better off, that fault is almost beside the point. But we are responsible. That is, we must respond to that "something," must make the best of it, must turn it to our profit, and the profit of our customers and investors.

What is that "something"? Everything I've said in this book goes to show that we are in the grip of a second managerial revolution, one that's very different from the first. The first was about a transfer of *power*. This one is about an access of *freedom*. Slowly, or suddenly, corporate managers all over the world are learning that free enterprise these days really is free. Markets are wide open: Anybody can play. Customers have money in their pockets, and brains in their heads: They're free, too, to pick and choose as they like. And so are businesses free— emancipated from the shackles of government control, regulation, and protection to seek opportunities wherever they can find them.

So why don't we hear more cheering and self-congratulation, of the sort that greeted the first managerial revolution? Because freedom is an ambiguous gift, is why. Businesses, and their managers with them, are free to succeed as never before; the opportunities of the new world market are dazzling, the potential rewards of success (think of China!) are truly mind-boggling. But opportunity, though we don't often admit it, is also, by definition, the opportunity to fail. Freedom, in other words, is a challenge, and endless freedom is an endless challenge.

Fundamentally, the "answer" of this book to the challenge of market freedom is . . . more freedom, *our* freedom. I mean the very specific forms of freedom embraced by reengineering. It's the freedom to zig and zag: to change our strategies, our work and management processes, our business purposes, our *minds*. It's the freedom at the center of the paradox of power: that the best way to *get* is to *let go*. It's the freedom at the heart of the dispersal of authority and accountability out to where the customers are. It's the freedom to get out there ourselves. It's the freedom without which we can never summon the ideas and images we need to meet the demands and opportunities of our markets. And it's more obvious sorts of freedom, too: freedom from stifling hierarchies, from organizational "slots" and "boxes," and from the corpse of memory (which actually looks like a rusty old machine).

That, finally, is the message of this book: Free markets need free men and women to invent the future.

INDEX